ESTHER THE
WONDER PIG

ESTHER THE WONDER PIG

Changing the World
One Heart at a Time

STEVE JENKINS AND DEREK WALTER

with Caprice Crane

G|C

GRAND CENTRAL
PUBLISHING

NEW YORK   BOSTON

Grand Central Publishing
Hachette Book Group
1290 Avenue of the Americas
New York, NY 10104

www.HachetteBookGroup.com

Printed in the United States of America

RRD-C

First Edition: May 2016

10 9 8 7 6 5 4 3 2

Grand Central Publishing is a division of Hachette Book Group, Inc. The Grand Central Publishing name and logo is a trademark of Hachette Book Group, Inc.

The Hachette Speakers Bureau provides a wide range of authors for speaking events. To find out more, go to www.hachettespeakersbureau.com or call (866) 376-6591.

The publisher is not responsible for websites (or their content) that are not owned by the publisher.

Library of Congress Cataloging-in-Publication Data has been applied for.

ISBN 978-1-4555-6078-3

To Esther. For giving us the strength and courage to follow our dreams. For making us laugh every single day, and for teaching us how to be kinder, more compassionate people. Our lives will never be the same because of you, and we can't imagine having it any other way.

To all the people who dedicate their lives to rescuing animals, and teaching others how easy it can be to live an "Esther Approved" lifestyle. Slowly but surely we can and we are making a difference.

And to the millions of Esthers around the world that haven't been so lucky. We're sorry, we love you, and we'll never stop working to give you a name.

ESTHER THE
WONDER PIG

CHAPTER ONE

There's little point to a life that lacks excitement. But there's excitement, and then there's a freight train hurtling toward your bedroom at 3 a.m. on a fairly regular basis.

We call it the Piggy Parade.

It sounds tame, but in reality there is nothing tame or serene about being startled awake by a 650-pound commercial pig barreling down your hallway. It's something you feel first: There's a vibration that starts to rumble through the mattress into your sleepy consciousness and you have just moments to realize what's happening and make room for a mammoth being who fully intends to make herself at home *on your bed*. Over the din of pillows flying and humans and dogs and cats alike all scrambling to get out of the way, comes the sound of hooves racing across the hardwood floor, gaining momentum with every step, getting louder by the second. Once you've heard that sound, it's embedded in your psyche, and your response is Pavlovian. (The term *Pavlovian*, having originated in reference to dogs, means that Reuben and Shelby, our beloved canines, also know what to do. Our cats, Delores and Finnegan, are on their own.) The sound is thunderous; the house practically shakes with each step—and there's the crash of the occasional piece of furniture getting knocked over. You hear it coming, you feel it in your bones, but there's nothing you can do.

Our darling princess comes crashing into the room, most likely spooked by a noise in the night. She launches into our bed much the same way she launched into our lives and while it might be a mad scramble to make room for her, it's also a whole new, wonderful level of exhilarating. And we wouldn't have it any other way.

Maybe pig parenting was my destiny. I've always loved animals. If I encountered a situation with a trapped dog and a trapped person, I hate to say it, but I feel I would help the animal first. Animals need humans to help them. And for whatever reason, I've always felt like their protector.

My very first best friend was my childhood dog, Brandy. She was a shepherd mix, brown and black with floppy ears and a long straight tail, a nice contrast to my super-light blond shaggy hair—though I didn't have the floppy ears and tail. (I looked a little like Dennis the Menace, and some might say we shared some personality traits as well. Though Steve the Menace doesn't quite have the same ring to it.) Brandy and I were inseparable. And she followed me like a shadow everywhere I went— to friends' houses, to the park, even from room to room in our home.

We lived in Mississauga, a fairly big city, but it was a different time: Life was simpler and safer then. We used to ride our bikes and walk everywhere until it was dark and thus time to go home.

Before we had any pets at our house, independent six-year-old that I was, I'd explore other yards to see what pets they had and occasionally find myself trespassing to make a new friend. My parents never let me forget the time I ignored the "home by dark" rule. I had made fast friends that day with a neighbor's dog, and at a certain point the family who lived there told me it was time to go home. So off I went, out the gate and out of sight. But when the family disappeared into their abode, I let myself back in and continued to play with the dog. When you're a kid you don't think about little things like "worried parents" or "breaking and entering."

My subterfuge was uncovered during a heated game of fetch: The stick that was thrown accidentally hit the window. (Do you like how I put that one on the stick, like I wasn't the one who threw it? That's just because I couldn't find a way to blame the dog.)

When the curtains opened and the couple peered out to see what the noise was, I stood very still. I tried to think of myself as a chameleon, hoping to blend in with their yard. Maybe I should have gone with ninja instead of chameleon, because that didn't work at all. Oddly, I was not invisible, and the kind woman came out and invited me into her house to play with the dog inside . . . where there would be no fetch or broken windows.

A heartwarming story, isn't it?

Funny how that all changes when the police come knocking on the door.

Yes, that's what happened. Apparently they were canvassing the neighborhood at the prompting of my panicked parents. (At least it's nice to know they cared.) I'd honestly been completely oblivious to the terror I was putting my parents through by not returning home on time, but you'd better believe I heard about it when I got home. Over and over until I went to sleep that night.

However, you *could* say that my little B&E was actually rewarded, because that very same week my parents got Brandy for me . . . so this would never happen again.

Whenever my parents went out of town, my paternal grandmother would stay with us. This is a woman who grew up in Scotland during World War II. I wouldn't exactly say she was a hard-ass, but I knew well enough that if Grandma said no, the answer was *no*. Still, I adored her. We always had a great relationship, though my healthy respect for her likely was why my parents felt safe leaving me in her care.

One day when my parents were away and Grandma was in charge, I went next door to our neighbors' house. For some reason, Grandma wouldn't let me take Brandy. I knew Brandy would be upset, but I also knew I couldn't argue with Grandma, so I left Brandy behind.

That was the last time I saw Brandy alive.

Since I was right next door, Brandy could hear my voice as I laughed and played with the other kids, and it drove her crazy. She wanted to be with me. She knew I was just one fence-hop away, so she tried to leap it. But her collar caught on the fence, and she hanged herself.

Thankfully, I didn't actually see her on the fence—I learned what happened from my parents—but even just knowing how it happened was too much. If you're reading this book, you're obviously an animal lover, and I'm sure that sad story was rough on you. You can imagine how hard it hit me, a child for whom Brandy was family.

Many of us have suffered the tragedy of having a beloved pet killed by a passing car, and I'm not taking anything away from how painful that is. But the circumstances of Brandy's death were just crushing. I couldn't get the image out of my mind: my girl hanging there limp and lifeless, and all just because she wanted to come play with me. It turned my insides out.

While most of my childhood memories are pretty fuzzy, this one sticks out clear as day. It's the first memory I have of being truly heartbroken and knowing I had lost something I'd never thought I'd lose. As I child, you don't think about the unfairly short lifespans of your pets—you assume this friend will be with you forever. But even if I had been prepared for the fact that some-day, maybe ten or fourteen years down the road, I might have to say goodbye to her, this had never been in the cards. To this day, thinking about her makes my eyes water.

The majority of my memories as a child are of vaca-tions or riding my bike around the lake near my house. And yes, my Dennis the Menace–like explorations of the neighborhood. Brandy's death is the one moment of gut-wrenching sadness I remember like it was yesterday, that sharp pain of loss coupled with feeling entirely to blame for her trying to join me next door. For months, I would wake up in the middle of the night and call out her name. I'd sob uncontrollably when I'd realize it wasn't a bad dream—Brandy was really *gone*. I felt so respon-sible. I think that's when I decided I would never aban-don any animal that needed me. I'm just plain drawn to animals. And just maybe it borders on a problem.

Before Esther, we were already two guys, one girl, two dogs, and two cats living in a 1,000-square-foot house in Georgetown—it was close quarters. Our house was a mod-est single-level home consisting of a combined living/din-ing/kitchen area and three bedrooms. Derek and I shared one bedroom, we had a roommate occupying another, and the remaining one became a makeshift office we all shared for our various needs: I used it to run my real estate business, Derek made phone calls to book his magic shows.

Our only TV was in the living room, but our living room was so small that on the rare occasion all three of us wanted to watch TV at the same time, there just wasn't enough room for everyone to sit. Not to mention we had two dogs who *also* required comfy seating—and removing them from one of the three available seats just didn't seem fair if you're living by "first come, first served" rules. As our policy *did* include the animals, this usually resulted in one or more humans sitting on the floor with a throw pillow at best.

We shared a single washroom, and if you've ever lived with roommates (or worse, *kids*) in a similar situation, you know how competitive that makes you. You'd hear footsteps in the morning and shoot out of bed, hoping to beat the other person to the punch. Otherwise you might have to wait twenty minutes for whoever was in there to finish up, and depending on your particular washroom needs at the moment, those could be twenty *long* minutes. This was one of the more challenging aspects of living in such close quarters. All too often, our schedules coincided in the worst possible way: I would have an urgent appointment, Derek had to get to a show—and everyone needed *that one room*. There was always somebody in a rush, and always somebody else who had to pee.

When we weren't competing for pole position to the potty, we bumped into one another a lot in the small living space. So we tried our best to give one another as much room as possible. I'd often take my laptop to the living room and work from there when Derek was in the office. We were in this configuration when I received a random Facebook message from a girl I dated in middle school, someone I hadn't spoken to in fifteen years.

> Hey Steve. I know you've always been a huge animal lover. I have a mini pig that is not getting along with my dogs. I've just had a baby and I can't keep the pig.

I was alone in the living room, immediately intrigued. I might have looked around to see if anyone else could see my computer screen or my gleeful expression. A mini pig? That sounds adorable. Who *wouldn't* want a mini pig?

In hindsight, yes, the whole situation was bizarre. I hadn't heard from this woman in over a decade. And now might be a good time to admit something. (And you'd better believe it will come up later.) I've always been *way* too trusting. I just kind of go with the flow. At the time, I didn't think, *Hey, this is really weird*. My thought process was more like, *Hey, it's Amanda, great to hear from her!* I didn't think about the strangeness of it all. The fact that she was offering me a mini pig just seemed neat.

There was no photo attached, so I was flying blind. But I didn't need a photo to know I was interested. I replied with a casual *Let me do some research and I'll get back to you*, but I immediately knew I wanted the pig—I just had to figure out how to make it happen.

It's tricky enough bringing a pig, even a mini pig, back to the home you share with your partner. And a roommate. And several other pets. But on top of that, only nine months earlier, I'd brought a new cat home without talking to Derek about it first. As you might expect, that didn't go well at all. (And it's not like I could blame anyone but myself.)

So I had to plan this right, to make it look like this wasn't something I was doing behind Derek's back, even though this was absolutely, totally, 100 percent something I was doing behind Derek's back. I had to make it seem like it wasn't something *I* did; the pig just kind of . . . happened.

Pigs just happen, right?

A few hours later, I got another message from Amanda:

Someone else is interested so if you want her great if not this other person will take her.

You're probably smart enough to recognize this as the manipulative tactic it was, and normally I'm smart enough too—I'm in real estate, after all. But when I want something, I have to have it—and that's when my IQ drops...how many points? Probably all of them.

I was not letting that pig go.

I don't know why. I hadn't even laid eyes on this little piggy, but I felt a panic over losing her. I thought I'd have more time to decide. I thought I'd maybe do some research and (maybe, possibly, you never know) even talk to Derek about it. I didn't think that two hours later I'd have to say yes or no. But there we were. A new message threatening to give this mini pig to someone else. So without thinking it through at all, I told Amanda I'd take the pig. I gave her my office address, and we agreed to meet there in the morning.

In my mind, I was mostly doing this just to get her to stop talking to the other interested person. If there even was another interested person. But again—these are the things you don't consider when you are as trusting a soul as I. (Also referred to in some circles as a complete sucker.)

Regardless, I agreed to meet with Amanda. I figured I'd do a little homework overnight. I knew nothing about mini pigs. I didn't know what they ate; I had no idea how big they got. So I started doing some Internet research. I found a few assertions that "There's no such thing as a mini pig." And yes, that should have been a red flag, but I was blinded by my faith in Amanda (and my sudden obsession with having a pet pig). I knew this person. I'd gone to school with her. She wasn't talking to a stranger. Amanda said it was a mini pig and I believed her, because why would she lie?

So that thing on the Internet was the only hiccup. Everything else I saw was *super cute*. It seemed this pig would grow to be about seventy pounds max. That was pretty close to the size of Shelby, one of our dogs. So I figured it would be another Shelby. Maybe a slightly *denser* Shelby. That seemed reasonable. And different! A pig!

That day, I told Derek I was going two hours north to the Kincardine Scottish Festival and Highland Games. I planned to do the "meet" at my office on my way out of town, and once I actually saw the porcine princess, I'd decide if this could actually work out and take it from there.

I *was* actually going to Kincardine—that part was true. It had been planned for two weeks before I'd even heard about the pig. The plan just got altered when she came into the picture, and it worked to my benefit, because it gave me time to sort it out. My plan was to tell Derek I found a pig on the way *home* from Kincardine. I mean, that could happen, right? One might potentially think he'd have expected such a thing after our having been together for so many years. Derek, more than anyone, is aware of my history with animals. And my history of bringing them home without discussing it with him in advance.

I booked a room in a hotel that was on the way to the festival, and my plan was to keep our new addition there for a few hours on Day One while I strategized. And had a few beers. And discussed it with my friends. And then I'd come back at night and sleep in the room with the pig and then do the same the next day until it was time to come home with my new pig and my perfectly formulated story. (I know. Sometimes my schemes are more complicated than the heist in *Ocean's Eleven*.)

But once I saw Esther and held her in my arms, that plan went out the window.

I'm getting ahead of myself. When Amanda pulled up there was no pig in sight, just a laundry basket on the passenger seat with a flannel blanket over the top. Amanda and I walked around to the side of the car; Amanda opened the door and pulled back the blanket.

There she was. Tiny. Staring up at me. Innocent. Precious. With pink nail polish on her little hooves? Ratty, chipped nail polish no less. This poor thing. She had a frayed sequined little cat collar around her neck with tattered threads hanging off it, and I thought, *How is this brand-new baby already such a hot mess?* She looked pathetic. Yet so lovable. And all I wanted to do was hold her. Immediately. But not outside where people could see and she might get scared. We covered the little girl back up and carried the laundry basket into my office, where I picked her up and held her for the very first time.

She was *tiny*—maybe eight inches from tip to tail. I could hold her in one hand. Honestly, the wee pig didn't look great. Her ears were completely sunburned. They reminded me of that scary "Tan Mom" lady or that fried-to-a-crisp woman in *There's Something About Mary*. But it was endearing, like a sad, wet puppy. Before I'd seen her, I thought this was just a cool idea. *A pet pig. Fun!* But when I saw her, I just thought, *Oh my God look what they've done to her.* I could see her little hipbones. And those ears! I knew I had to heal those ears, and I also knew I already loved this pig.

Amanda said the pig was six months old and spayed. She said she'd had her for a week. She got her from a breeder on Kijiji (an online marketplace similar to Craigslist). I watched Amanda handle the pig and listened to the way she talked about her and I could tell there was *zero* attachment on Amanda's part. It was hard to even take that in, and it frightened me. I didn't know *what* Amanda would do if I didn't accept this piglet and send Amanda on her way.

So I did.

But this changed everything. And not just in the grand

scheme of my life. My original plan on how to handle Derek, with all its carefully conceived machinations, was now shot. Because I loved this pig. I had known her for a total of twelve minutes and already I had an instinctual love for her that said, *You can't just leave this girl in a hotel room for hours while you're off partying at a festival.* She was a baby. She needed me.

I canceled my trip north and now had to prepare *two* stories for Derek: Why wasn't I in Kincardine? And why did I bring home a *pig*? My original plan positioned me as a hero. I was the good guy. *I saved this piglet! Of course, I didn't want to take her, but what could I do?* I had been totally confident with my cover story...and then karma bit me in the ass.

I'd thought I would have a couple of days and access to a bunch of friends who would help me fine-tune my story and now that was all blown to hell because I was head-over-heels in love with a pig. I had to see Derek that same day, and I only had a few hours to figure this out.

That's when the pressure really started.

I called the friends who were expecting me in Kincardine to tell them I wasn't coming and why, which they all thought was hilarious. They knew Derek would freak out, so they wanted me to keep them posted. They gave me two instructions: One, send them a photo of the pig. Two, send them a photo of Derek's reaction.

Then I called our friends Erin and Wally. I needed

them to watch the pig while I went emergency grocery shopping to make the fancy "please forgive me for getting a pig" dinner that I would now be making for Derek. I didn't actually say, "I need you to watch a pig." I believe I just said I needed them to pet-sit, so they had no idea what I was bringing to their house until I showed up at their door and the little piglet scurried out onto their kitchen floor. Erin was flabbergasted. I believe her first words were: "Holy shitballs, Derek is going to murder you." Derek and Erin actually dated in high school, so she knows him almost as well as I do.

Once I'd done my shopping, I reclaimed the pig. In the car, she sat on the front seat beside me, looking nervous and disoriented. I talked to her and petted her while we took the small back roads to our house. I brought her inside and put the dogs outside. We sat together, just the two of us, in the living room for a while as I tried to think of what to feed her. (Something I forgot to do in all of this was to figure out what a pig would eat and make a point of actually *getting* it.) So I gave her lettuce, dog food, tomatoes, anything I could think of. She settled on lettuce and rabbit food.

Once I knew she had something in her system, I got to work cleaning up a little and making dinner. I figured the best use of my time would be to clean the house from top to bottom, make my nice dinner, and have it be like Derek was coming home to this great romantic gesture.

I kept the dogs away initially so the pig could get comfy. The cats were their typical curious-but-uninterested selves. Once I did let the dogs see her, I was careful to hold her securely, not letting them get too close at first. Shelby and Reuben are both super excitable around baby animals and children, so there was a ton of whining and jumping up. I let them sniff her a little and even get in a few friendly licks before I hid her in the office down the hall. I figured I'd better get Derek in a good mood before springing the new arrival on him. Also, the other animals were a bit confused, so I decided to keep everyone separate for a while.

I cleaned the best I could in the tighter-than-tight timeframe and then cooked my special dinner, Derek's favorite: fresh burgers with cheese and bacon, with homemade garlic fries. The scene was set. Wine was poured. I lit some candles to really sell the ambiance. And there I waited...

CHAPTER TWO

It was about 8:30 p.m., and I knew Derek would be exhausted after a long day of magic shows, and this was probably not going to be the best time to spring something of this magnitude on him, but I had no choice. And no matter how delightful a homecoming I crafted to ease him into my exciting news, there was already a "tell" in the fact that I was even *there*. I was supposed to be at the festival, so the minute he saw my car he would know something was up. I was so nervous. I kept pacing around the house, running my story through my head as I tried to make sure the entire place was spotless and everything was perfect. I tried to think of every possible scenario and the reactions Derek might have and then constructed my responses for each. I imagined this was probably what playing chess was like, anticipating my opponent's next move and then calculating mine. Tactical warfare. And this is why I never played chess. Not to mention, this wasn't really my opponent—he wasn't a pawn here—this was my *partner*, and the only way to win this game was if we both were happy. So I paced and imagined every possible wonderful or terrible thing that would happen until I heard Derek's car pull in the driveway. Then I just took a deep breath.

When Derek walked through the door and took one look around, I could tell alarms were ringing in his head. First of all, the entire house was clean. We're not untidy, but it's not like Derek came home every day to a home that looked like a real estate agent was showing it off for prospective buyers. I do my best to be a good partner and do a lot of work around the house, but cleaning and making dinner: definitely not my forte. Especially cleaning. Derek has been known to say that wherever I go, I leave lids, caps, notes, you name it—you can pretty much *CSI* wherever I've been by the trail I've left behind. *He took his hat off over here, he put his keys over there, he sat there and had a drink while he watched TV.* But on this night, our house looked staged for sale. This was *really* out of the norm. Also, I had made us dinner. I *never* made dinner. Derek traditionally did all the cooking, and there was a good reason for that. On the rare occasions when I tried to cook, it was because I'd seen some crazy recipe I was determined to attempt. And 99.9 percent of the time, I failed miserably, just like those epic cooking fails everyone laughs at on Pinterest. Yet there I was, innocently standing next to the only thing I knew how to make.

I couldn't have made my guilt more obvious if I'd tried.

Derek had a show bag in one hand and a rabbit carrier in the other. In less than fifteen seconds, his face betrayed his suspicion. He knew we had a situation.

"What's going on?" he said. I tried to hand him a glass of wine, totally nonchalant, as if our entire life weren't about to completely—and drastically—change. My heart was in my throat as his *What's going on?* echoed in my head. I tried to come up with my answer. So much for all of my run-throughs. You would have thought I'd be prepared for such an obvious question, but all my preparation seemed to have suddenly evaporated.

The notorious boxer Mike Tyson has a saying: Everybody has a plan until they get punched in the mouth. And while I wouldn't call myself a fan, I must admit to feeling something very similar to what Mr. Tyson said. I just didn't expect those narrowed eyes and furrowed brow right off the bat! It made me wonder if maybe Derek had spoken to Erin and Wally. I had told them not to tell, but how could I know if they really hadn't? What if Erin had given him a heads-up? I had no idea.

"I changed my mind," I said. "Just didn't want to go away. Wasn't really in the mood to party."

"*Really,*" Derek answered, the tiniest hint of a smirk creeping onto his face, like he believed that as much as he would have believed me if I'd just told him the Food Network wanted to give me my own cooking show. (Which, by the way, would be hilarious if they ever decided they were interested in comedy.) He knew I loved going to Kincardine. He knew I always looked forward to this particular weekend.

He knew I was lying.

But before I could even continue to unwind my well-rehearsed string of lies, something caught his eye. He looked down the hallway and noticed Shelby and Reuben perched outside the office, looking through the French doors into that room. That door is never closed, and the dogs are never seated at the end of the hallway.

Derek knew then and there that whatever situation I was trying to butter him up for was happening at the end of that hallway. I scrambled for the right words but in that moment, my mind went completely blank. And he wasn't the type to sit tight while I worked up the courage and worked down his defenses—undoubtedly using several glasses of wine for both strategies—to divulge something he wanted to know *now*. I just stood in horror, knowing he was seconds away from seeing our newest family member.

Derek charged down the hallway, with me protesting and chasing after him, and trying not spill my wine.

He swung open the door to the office and just stood there like a statue, one hand on the door frame, the other still on the handle. Every emotion other than happiness flashed across his face in a matter of seconds. He didn't even look at me. I'm sure he wanted to; I saw his eyes darting around as he took in the situation, but for the most part he kept his eyes on the pig, his body stiff with tension. He looked like he was a combination of shocked, horrified, and furious. I had known he would be upset, but I didn't know *how* upset. I was partially bracing myself for him to say she had to go. I wasn't sure how the next few minutes were going to play out. His family has always had a flair for dramatics, so I wasn't sure if there was going to be a blowout that ended with his storming out, or if he would admit the fact that it was super cool and be as excited as I was. (Yes, the latter was an entirely optimistic and almost certainly unbelievable scenario, but one can hope, right?)

"Huh," Derek said. "There's a pig in my home. No way on earth was I expecting *that*."

And there she was, a wee little pig, her little tiny feet scurrying around.

For our new addition, this was a brand-new environment, and she was pretty sketched out. Every time I opened the door she would try to run, but her little hooves would slip around on the floor and spin out like the Road Runner's before takeoff—just a blur of tiny legs, flying in every direction. She'd done this a few times when I checked in on her as I was cooking. She'd fire up those little legs, sprint in place for a second, and then slide around the room until she found a safe place to hide: the chair, her cat carrier, my filing cabinet. Then moments later, that little snout would lead the way as she peeked out to say hello. It was adorable.

I was just hoping Derek would realize how much adorable was happening right before his very eyes.

Of course, it didn't take more than a half-second for him to know what I had done, why she was here, and what I had planned. Another pet, another addition to *our* home—and a *pig*, no less.

He was furious. Before I could get out a single syllable of explanation, he turned to me.

"No way. There is no way whatsoever we are having another animal. There is no fucking way that we are keeping a pig. There is no more room at the inn!"

His shouting turned to laughter. Like he started thinking, *This must be a joke. Steve's just pulling a prank, right? He can't* possibly *be this foolish.*

(Oh, believe me, I can.)

And then the reality set in for Derek: *Shit, Steve really is this foolish.*

"We just got Delores nine months ago!" he reminded me, as if I didn't know. "Are we on a cycle? Were you gestating this pig from the day I finally said yes to the cat?"

That might sound like a joke, but he was not joking; he was furious. He slammed the door and went straight to our bedroom to change out of his show outfit, throwing his clothes on the bed, yanking shirts off hangers, slamming dresser drawers. This was the dramatic flair that definitely didn't skip a generation in Derek's family.

I approached the door, attempting the tried-and-true "Babe, it's fine" routine, but he just ranted and raved about how irresponsible I was and how disrespectful it was for me to do this without asking him. He also (correctly) pointed out the fact that neither of us knew how to care for a piglet. The only positive thing I could say that wasn't a lie was, "She's a mini pig! She'll stay small!"

Well, at least it wasn't a lie as far as I knew at the time.

Derek didn't wake up any happier the next day. He didn't want to look at her, hold her, or have anything to do with her. It was two days before he would even touch her, and he only did that because I shoved her into his arms. He made threats: "It's me or the pig." He didn't mean it, of course: He's always said he would never leave me, and I believe it. It was just a scare tactic, and it didn't work. But things remained tense. To put it mildly.

I knew I was in the wrong, so I went out of my way to stay upbeat, be on my best behavior, and remain positive. Whenever a new situation arose—and let's face it, this was *all* new—I'd just be lighthearted and try to reassure Derek that things were totally copacetic. My internal and external mantra was a steady course of *It's okay* and *It'll be fine*, alternately applied to me trying to convince Derek to accept the pig, and me trying to convince myself this would all work out.

Derek hadn't signed up for this, and my hope that he'd come around to thinking a pig was an awesome idea was dwindling as each day passed. This wasn't a simple "I'm mad at you" situation. There was nothing typical about this scenario. Derek's anger wasn't abating anytime soon. The way I'd originally figured it in my head, he would get just a *little bit* upset with me, but then he'd fall in love with the pig. It was not falling into place as I'd hoped and anticipated. I knew I was pushing my luck, but I hadn't expected him to be anywhere near as angry as he was. This was as angry as I'd ever seen him, and I was starting to think he might actually force me to give her up without even giving her a chance. Then that spiraled into me imagining my reaction to him kicking our new baby pig out into the cold, heartless world, and I was suddenly creating scenarios that got worse and worse.

But the worst part of it all was the one thing Derek kept saying over and over: "It's not 'the pig.' It's how you did it and that you did it behind my back." It was the whole "I'm not mad, I'm disappointed" thing, except he *was* mad *and* disappointed and he had a right to both of those feelings. It was brutal. I knew I was wrong and I felt awful about it, but I tried to maintain at least a glimmer of hope that I could smooth things over. I loved Derek and I loved our life together, and I believed that once he got over the shock and annoyance of the initial deception, he'd eventually come around.

And then in the midst of all the drama and the fighting, maybe a week or so later, Derek fell in love. He was head over heels for a pig, of all things, experiencing all the firsts you have with a new pet.

Back when I had sprung Delores on Derek, he refused to give her a "real" name at first. In the same way, he started off referring to the pig as Kijiji. He wasn't going to give a name to this animal we weren't keeping (or so he thought). But two weeks in, he stopped calling her Kijiji, and we gave her a real name. I'm not sure why we chose it, but we wanted a name for a wise old soul, and "Esther" felt right. And she responded to it well, so it stuck.

I knew Derek would fall in love with Esther. He talks a good game, but he's really a softie. And come on, who wouldn't love Esther? Here was this two-pound little wiggler with what we could already tell was a giant personality. Thankfully, she was a mini pig and wouldn't grow that big.

At least that's what we thought. Wow, were we naïve. Okay, *I* was naïve.

But in hindsight, I'm glad we didn't know. I don't think we would have kept her if we'd had any idea what was in store for us. For starters, we were taking on a task that didn't follow any kind of rulebook. I mean, you won't happen upon *Raising Commercial Pigs in Your House for Dummies* in your local Barnes & Noble, because it doesn't exist. With good reason. There's nothing simple about having a pet pig—it's not like having a "normal" domestic pet, or even a child. We had no idea about the complexities of "piggy-proofing" a house (pigs are far more ingenious than you'd ever expect) or how to find a pig sitter when we needed to travel. It's pretty easy to ask someone to check on the cats every day or so or to put dogs in a kennel. But there isn't a ready chain of piggy play centers one can rely on in a pinch. And don't even get me started on pigs' personalities and piggy mood swings (or PMS!).

If someone had told me up front all the life changes that were coming, I might have thrown my arms in the air and said, *Forget it!* But Esther had us under a spell. We fell more in love with her every day, so every time something came up, we found a way to deal with it (or justify the things we couldn't change) and just carried on. Once we fell for her, that was that: Esther was part of the family.

It's a funny thing how the official decision was made. We were having dinner one night and Derek just started talking about things that were much more long-term sounding than anything we'd ever discussed: "Where will her litter go? Where should we build her a pen?" These things definitely sounded permanent. You don't "build a pen" for someone you're getting rid of. That's when I started beaming inside. That's when I knew he was really on board.

"So we're keeping her?" I asked with a big dumb smile on my face, but I had my answer, and I was ecstatic.

Of course, even when we all thought Esther was a mini pig, our parents were entirely confused by the situation. Derek's parents had had to come around to our being a couple, and now this family of hunters and farmers were supposed to accept that we were living with a pig? As a pet?

They thought we were insane. Pigs are food! Pigs are dirty! (In truth, she's not really dirty—she actually smells pretty amazing.)

They tried to be supportive, but they really didn't get it at all. Derek's family said things like, *Grandma can't believe you have a pig* and *Grandpa is rolling in his grave that you have a pig in the house.*

I can't pretend this didn't sting a little at first. Life presents enough challenges without having to worry about whether you have the support of your families. I tried really hard to get the approval of Derek's parents, and I know their opinion meant a lot to Derek whether he showed it or not. More than once I wanted to talk to Derek about it, to push him. To get him to stand up for us and defend what we were doing. But I never did. Looking at the big picture, Derek's family had come such a long way and accepted so many things about us—like the fact that we were gay—that I just accepted this would take more time. And I had to admit that it was easy to see why people would think we were crazy. We let them say what they wanted. We knew they'd eventually come around.

While Derek's parents were (understandably) baffled, my mom was a little more go-with-the-flow about the whole thing. After years of watching her son fall in love with every animal from here to eternity, it wasn't all that surprising that one day I'd come home with a pig.

Derek did insist on one thing: Because I'd brought Esther into our home, most of the responsibility would be mine. Between walking the dogs and cleaning up after them—and cleaning up after me—he'd had enough.

We were in the kitchen, deciding what we wanted to eat for dinner, when Esther looked up at us sweetly and peed on the floor. Of course I felt guilty the minute she did it, and I knew she didn't mean to (and Derek knew that too), but that didn't mean it wasn't a giant pain in the ass. A few moments passed.

"You're going to need to take care of that," he said. And I planned to, of course, but I hadn't jumped on it right at that second. I guess I was just taken by surprise.

"Of course," I replied, grabbing the paper towels and wiping up the mess.

"I mean, not just right now," Derek clarified. "You brought her home without discussing it with me, and if we're going to keep her, she's going to be your responsibility."

"I get it," I said, motioning to indicate the fact that I was on my hands and knees. "This is me taking responsibility."

"You'll walk her; you'll clean up after her; you'll feed her."

I felt like a child being read the rules by Dad before getting my first puppy. It was like I was being given something that could be taken away if I wasn't a good boy. But that also meant I'd get to keep her if I *was* a good boy.

"Okay!" I beamed.

"Okay," he said, and for some time after that, I did most of Esther's caretaking. It was fine with me. If that was all it took to let us keep Esther, I was happy to do it. I'd deal with her messes. And I did pretty well with it.

But even when Esther was small, housetraining her was difficult, and we soon were going through a metric ton of paper towels. I kept coming up with ideas to keep her contained. First, I found a kids' playpen for sale (on Kijiji of all places) and bought it. That worked for about a week before it was saturated in urine. So then I moved her into a big dog crate with her little litter box and some blankets to bed down in. It had a plastic base, so it was easier to clean. I tried to keep up on messes before Derek saw them and discreetly hide the evidence deep in the garbage to keep up the impression that I had everything under control. I wanted to show him how incredibly easy and carefree it was to have a tiny piggy. Once we realized we could have wiped out a rain forest with all the paper towels we were using, we adapted and bought reusable, washable towels. Not only was it more cost-effective, but it was also much better for the environment.

Because Esther was my responsibility, I took her to the vet the first time she went. Doing some online research about toilet training pigs, I stumbled across a pig breeder in Orangeville, a small town about an hour northwest of Georgetown. Their vet talked to me for quite a while about techniques we could try, all of which I felt we had already exhausted. She also said that based on what I was telling her, there was a chance Esther might have kidney stones, apparently a common condition in pigs. This vet referred me to another vet whose practice was just a bit south of Orangeville, in Caledon. Apparently he had a lot of experience with mini pigs, or at least much more experience than our current vet had. I knew pigs were different from cats and dogs, obviously, so I wanted someone who had experience with pigs.

I loaded Esther into a cat carrier and away we went in my car. She was hidden by the carrier so it was super discreet. Nobody could've known she was there. I don't know who I thought might be looking or why I needed to keep her a secret, but I guess I just didn't want to make a spectacle. I put her in the middle of the car so I could see her the whole time, and there was her little face, looking back at me, seeming quite happy to go for a ride. I was pretty excited on this first vet trip, because I was so sure he would say, "Yup, she's got stones. We'll treat it and your pee problems will be over." Simple as that. That was my attitude going in that day: complete optimism. *This whole pee thing was just a blip. My mini pig will be perfect and barely ever pee anywhere at all.*

Esther was still tiny then, but as soon as the veterinarian saw her, he looked up at me, head cocked, a bemused look on his face.

"What do you know about this pig?" he asked.

Huh. That sounded a bit ominous.

I gave the doctor the story—or at least the story I'd been told.

"Okay, well, already I see a problem in your story. Look at her tail."

I looked at her tail. I didn't know what I was supposed

to be noticing. This was my first foray into pig tails. But I acted like I was examining it nonetheless.

"Her tail has been 'docked,'" he said.

"Is that why it's a little nub?" I asked.

"Exactly," he said. "When you have a commercial pig—that's a full-size pig—the owners will generally have the pig's tail cut back substantially. This minimizes tail-biting, a behavior that occurs when pigs are kept deprived in factory farm environments."

Well, all of that sounded terrible, but I wasn't sure what it had to do with Esther or why some monster had cut off her little tail. I wasn't getting it. And this veterinarian wasn't necessarily *saying* it...but it was hanging in the air.

"If the story your friend told you was true—that Esther really is six months old—she could just be a runt."

This threw me.

"You think she *lied*?" I asked, trying to wrap my head around the potential deceit. "I know this person."

"And I don't. So you could very well have a runt—"

Please don't call my baby girl a runt...

"—and my suspicions could be over nothing. If that's the case, when fully grown, she very well could be about seventy pounds."

"Okay," I said. I mean, that's what I thought she was going to be. No news here.

"But if not...I guess we'll cross that bridge when we get to it."

The doctor explained that the only way to know anything for sure would be to weigh and measure her and start a growth chart. He said pigs have a very specific rate of growth. He'd be able to compare Esther's growth to a standard chart and see where she fell. That would give us a better idea of her age and let us keep track of how she grew.

Over the next couple of months, we got to know Esther and settled into as much of a normal routine as we could. We still found ourselves marveling at the fact that we had a little piglet in the house. People came to visit and we'd laugh as we watched her scurry around or sleep in one of her many positions. Her favorite was having her feet and face buried in the heat vents on the floor. She would pop out the vent cover and literally press herself right into the vent.

We took her for walks late at night with the dogs. At the time, she was still smaller than both of them, so she could blend in if people on the street didn't look too closely. People occasionally noticed that we were walking a pig, and they would sometimes stop and ask questions, but most of the time we made it out and back without anything spectacular happening. Walks did prove to be challenging, because all Esther wanted to do was dig up the grass at the edge of the sidewalks—something our dogs never did, as they don't have that innate desire, so it was a learning curve that involved a lot of pulling on the leash. But we did it. We were handling it. We went for walks as a family and things were under control.

On our next vet visit, I had to admit, Esther had been growing *awfully* quickly. Over that short time, she'd started closing in on eighty pounds, which was already in excess of the seventy pounds I'd originally been told her maximum weight would be.

I had tried to get Esther's previous vet records—to make sure, among other things, that she'd been spayed—but Amanda had gone radio silent. There was a scar on Esther's belly that would have been consistent with her having been spayed, but we didn't have any confirmation. I reached out to Amanda again because it was actually a health concern: If Esther hadn't been spayed, she could develop tumors later in life. But Amanda dodged my inquiries again, which should have been telling.

Looking back, Amanda's intentionally ignoring my texts and emails was a pretty clear-cut indicator that she realized I was catching on: I'd been duped. I tried to reach her a few times, never indicating we were mad or anything, just asking for info about the breeder and trying to confirm whether Esther was spayed. I tried to be optimistic, but in my gut, I knew something was up. I still didn't honestly believe Esther was a commercial pig, but I knew there was more to the story than I had been told. Of course I downplayed it to Derek, but my wheels were turning. Why was Amanda so easy to reach before I picked Esther up, and now...nothing?

With no response from Amanda, we had two choices. Cutting Esther open was risky. Pigs are very hard to operate on, because they don't respond well to general anesthesia. An operation would potentially be nothing more than exploratory surgery, and who wants to cut their baby open? The other option was to wait until she was older and see if she started getting her cycle, which would come with its own challenges. Unspayed pigs go into heat monthly and can become very aggressive. If we waited, she actually could become dangerous to us, and by that time surgery would be even *more* dangerous to her. Pigs get fatty as they develop, and at that point the risk of accidentally cutting an artery or a vein becomes higher. And if that happens, it can be hard to locate the source of the bleeding, and she could bleed out.

There were risks either way. It was a phenomenally hard decision, and we struggled with it for a long time. By this point, Derek and I loved Esther. I mean, I loved her the minute I saw her, but my feelings had grown into a deep, meaningful love. She was a member of our family. Derek was on the same page. He put up a strong face but he loved her as much as I did.

Ultimately, we decided against the surgery, and we wonder to this day whether we made the right call.

But that led to the conversation about the elephant in the room—or the pig in the room, as it were. The vet said that if Esther truly was six months old when we got her and actually was a runt, we still could expect her to grow to be 250 pounds.

And that was the *best-case* scenario.

The other scenario was that Esther was not a six-month-old runt when we got her. (Fine: when *I* got her.) Instead, it could turn out that we adopted her at just six *weeks* old, and she was no runt, but well on her way to being a full-size commercial pig. And at this growth rate, her ultimate full size was anyone's guess.

I was trying to wrap my mind around this distressing news. Everything was slowly adding up to the possibility that I'd gone out and adopted a commercial pig, and she could become enormous. I'd acquired Esther under Amanda's false pretenses, sure, but that wasn't making me feel any better.

Right there in the vet's office, I started Googling pictures on my phone. I was trying to get an idea of what a 250-pound pig looked like. I couldn't even fathom the size. Two hundred and fifty pounds would be a giant human being. Thankfully I found that pigs are really dense, so they are smaller than a human would be at the same weight. Still, 250 pounds makes for a very large pet, no matter how you look at it. And I was still trying to wrap my head around the possibility that she had not been spayed and would become aggressive for a week every month. Now I was supposed to understand that we might have an angry 250-pound bulldozer running around our little 1,000-square-foot house? The whole situation was very upsetting. And how was I supposed to explain all of this to Derek? He'd eventually come around to my latest surprise adoption, of a pig, no less, but he had no idea she could outgrow either of *us*. (Much less, as we'd find out down the line, both of us *combined*.)

I guess we could have paid more attention to everyone else's reactions, but it really hadn't fazed us when people would come over and say, "Holy Christ, she's huge!"

We saw Esther every day, so we weren't noticing it, as strange as that undoubtedly sounds. It's like the way you don't notice when you gain weight or your spouse does. (At least you'd better *pretend* you don't notice.) But we honestly weren't noticing, because this was all new to us. Come to think of it, Michelle, one of my best friends, did call Esther "Boss Hogg." Maybe we'd just been convincing ourselves it wasn't happening. Denial can be a powerful drug.

These were all the issues running through my mind as I headed home with Esther from the vet's office. I knew Derek and I had to talk.

When this sort of thing comes up, I always give Derek the best-case scenario. I get into the worst-case scenario only if he absolutely needs to know. And I knew he wasn't ready to hear this one. And if that sounds like I was being a little bit chickenshit about it, okay, guilty as charged.

I stopped off on my way home to buy Derek's favorite wine, a shiraz, in an effort to soften the potential blow— or at least get him drunk for it. We were seated on the couch with Esther between us, her head resting on a cushion. I was totally honest about the spay conversation, though, and we both shared our concerns. I used that to segue to the size situation.

"By the way," I started. "The doctor mentioned that Esther might grow a little bigger than we thought."

He cocked an eyebrow but said nothing. Of course then I got nervous and tried soft-pedaling the truth.

"There's a chance that she's actually *not* a mini pig."

"What kind of chance?" he asked.

"Well there's a good chance she'll grow bigger, because, I mean, she's already outgrown where we thought she'd be at her full-grown size."

Derek looked at her, taking in her already vast little self. "She is . . . larger than she should be."

"So," I continued, "I just wanted to be totally honest with you."

I know, I know.

"So how big?" he asked.

"A hundred pounds, maybe 120 . . . not a huge deal."

He sighed heavily, and his shoulders sunk down a little. He didn't seem mad; he seemed worried. I was grasping at straws, and he knew it. I was doing my typical, "It'll be fine," but Derek's initial facial reaction was completely "I told you so." And then, in a moment of perfect timing times a thousand, Esther lifted her head and rested it back down on Derek's leg, her gentle eyes looking up at him. *Good going, Esther!*

He laughed to himself and just shook his head. I fully expected him to lose it. He certainly deserved to lose it. I'm still counting my blessings that he handled it as well as he did. There definitely was an air of concern, but he gave me the benefit of the doubt. (Whereas what I deserved was a hell of a lot of doubt.) I think it was because he had already fallen in love with her. He knew that even if she grew, we couldn't just give her up. No matter how mad he was when Esther initially arrived, once she was in and accepted as part of the family, that was it. Realistically speaking, I'm not sure I would've gotten the same reaction had I been completely honest and told him *all* of the vet's concerns regarding her size. What I was describing to him was an average large dog, but in my heart, I was horrified.

Of course, I was keeping all that inside. I think in my gut I knew even then that she would turn out to be a commercial pig, but I swear I never thought she would get *this* big. Three hundred pounds maybe. But I didn't care. No matter how big she got, I was keeping her. I just had to downplay it all and hope nobody noticed.

As I said, denial is a powerful drug.

It was around this time that Esther was really starting to come into her own. She was playful. She wanted to cuddle. She was even playing with the dogs' toys. And we just loved her so much.

If you've never had a pet pig—and I'm sure that's the case for most people—this might not make any sense to you. But pigs are just as affectionate and caring and familial as any dog or cat you'll find. (Frankly, more so than *some* cats.)

I've never met anyone who can resist going nuts over baby animals. I'm like that and then some. In my mind I've always imagined my house as having one or two of everything. It's just a desire to know and touch and be with an animal. But I can't lie: The fact that Esther was a pig made me a little more excited than usual from the get-go. Hardly anyone had pigs for pets when we got Esther. (And it's not like they're giving dogs and cats a run for their money even now.) She was unique—an animal I had never interacted with before—and the thought of having a pig at home was incredible to me. To be honest, it could've been anything out of the ordinary and I think I would've been just as excited. For example, I've always wanted a monkey. I would have died to have a pet monkey. I hadn't *known* I'd wanted a pig, but the joy I felt after we had her and once I knew I would always be going home to a pig in my house—it just made me smile.

Having Esther was just so different, and there were many firsts. We'd notice her little quirks, the way she shuffled around, the way her little hooves slid along the floor when she ran, or just the funny little clicking noise she made when she pranced around. She was precious. She also snorted and farted way more than the dogs, which was less precious, but it *was* hilarious. Another thing that was completely different from any animals we'd ever had: She'd nuzzle our hands. That somehow comforted her or helped her calm down. It seemed to make her feel safe to know we were right there and that she could touch us. She would lick our palms and rub her snout up and down as she fell asleep. How does your heart not burst into a million pieces over that? She was adorable.

With any pet, the first time it makes a particular sound or moves in a specific way or just looks you in the eyes, you're trying to glean the meaning. You want to understand what this animal—now your pet, now your *family member*—is thinking and feeling, because you care. And you want your pet to know you care, that you'll do anything for it, just as you would for anyone else in your family, anyone you loved.

As soon as you start opening your heart to a creature, you start opening your mind to all the possibilities of what it's trying to tell you. You look for meaning in behaviors. Is that squeal a squeal of delight, of fear, of hunger, of surprise? Is that tilt of the head suggesting curiosity, concern, or confusion? Will she let me know when she isn't feeling well, and will I be perceptive enough to get it?

One thing I didn't expect was how many behaviors she would share with the dogs. She'd play with the dogs' toys the same way they would, picking a toy up and shaking it back and forth. Like the dogs, she'd want to cuddle when she was tired, climbing into our laps to nuzzle. To give us kisses, she'd stick her tongue out just a half an inch or so and then rub her head up and down against our hands.

And just like the dogs, she often wanted attention. She'd push her way closer to make sure you would pet her. If another one of the dogs or cats was getting attention, Esther wanted attention too. Of course, she wasn't able to sneak up on you like a cat, because she lacked the stealth. Frankly, she lacked *any* stealth. (Not exactly a prime candidate for the ninja academy is the commercial pig.)

It's hard to think that a 100-pound pig with cloven hooves on a hardwood floor would do extra things for your attention—just in case you somehow forgot she was there. But Esther did. And she probably wasn't unique in this.

That was when we really started to get it. She was special to us, yes—we adored her—but any other pig would have its own personality. Pigs undoubtedly have their own quirks and personalities, just like the hundreds of millions of dogs out there. We didn't do anything special to train her or turn her into what she was becoming. All we did was treat her like one of the dogs. She started playing and doing all these other hilarious and clever things all on her own. We could see the glimmer in her eyes and the little change in her facial expressions when she was chasing the cats or shaking one of the dogs' toys. The more we saw her with the rest of our furry family, the more she started to "look" like them. Not in a physical way, but in a personality and character kind of way. And that hit us deep in our cores.

What made pigs different? Why were they bred for food and held in captivity, while dogs and cats were welcomed into our homes and treated like family? Aside from physicality, we could see no difference between her and our dogs. (Okay, Esther hardly had any tail left to wag. But if it *had* been there, it would have been happily wagging away most of the time.)

Why were pigs the unlucky ones? Why didn't we

STEVE JENKINS AND DEREK WALTER

know previously they had such engaging personalities and such intelligence? And where would Esther be now if she hadn't come home with us?

We'd ponder such things many times over the years, but really, most of the time we were just happy to have our sweet, loving, oinking girl join our family. We'd never thought we were missing anything before—Derek even more than I, naturally—but now we couldn't fathom having a home without her. She's as integral to our home as the foundation, the walls, and the floors beneath our feet.

Floors that she'd soon be peeing all over. And I mean *all over*. But we'll get back to that in a bit.

CHAPTER THREE

It was a night in late September, I think. We'd had Esther for only a few weeks. I was at the computer; Derek was cooking dinner. We usually ate dinner around 7 p.m. I'd always have the TV on in the background when Derek cooked, but I'd sit close by at the dining room table with my computer to keep him company while *Seinfeld* or *King of the Hill* would ramble away in the background. The dining room overlooked the kitchen, separated by a counter, but otherwise they were right on top of each other. So I'd sit there where we could talk and I could see, hear, and smell everything he was doing.

Fall was a pretty good time for the real estate market where we lived, so I was fairly busy running around and getting new listings up before winter kicked in and things inevitably slowed down. Derek has an awesome eye for design and great style, so he's always been a huge help to my real estate business. He has helped me stage my listings, and we often discuss my feature sheets (the little flyer with photos for buyers to take when they view the property) and how they should be laid out. Another reason I think we make a great team.

On this particular night, we were having breakfast for dinner, something every adult should do on occasion—because you *can*. I was at the dining table, working on a feature sheet for a new listing. Derek was at the stove, Esther by his feet, wondering what he was cooking. (Just like a dog, as I said.) And I was watching them both. Esther would always honk, squeal, oink, and wag her tail when we were cooking because she wanted some of the food. And we weren't the best disciplinarians—we were known to share on occasion.

So there we were as Derek prepared the meal. He started to gather everything we needed for our breakfast sandwiches: toasted English muffins, cheese, eggs, and of course...bacon.

In the time we'd had Esther in our lives, we'd been eating the same way we'd eaten before her arrival. We had burgers. We had pepperoni on pizza. But we hadn't had bacon in a while. It hadn't been a conscious decision. We just hadn't had bacon. The connection hadn't even occurred to us.

On this particular evening, however, Derek was cooking bacon.

And suddenly something switched in my brain.

I recalled our vet specifically referring to Esther as a "commercial" pig, meaning her intended lot in life was to be food. That's the only purpose for a commercial pig. They don't pull sleds through the Yukon or carriages through the park. They become pork chops and ham hocks and link sausages and...

...yeah.

I heard the bacon crackling on the stove. The unmistakable scent wafted toward me. That smell, so wonderful to me (and let's be honest, to all carnivores) for my whole life up to that point suddenly smelled like something awful.

Like death.

I watched Derek cook, glanced at Esther's happy face, took in the whole scene. Derek was looking at the stove and occasionally down at sweet, happy, oinking Esther. If I could read her thoughts, and I'm pretty sure I could at that point, they'd go something like this:

Hey, Dad! Whatcha cookin' up there on that stove, and are you making enough for me?

Oh my God.

What were we doing?

When you eat meat every day (or at least most days), you try to justify it to yourself every step of the way. Or at least you do if you're me—I know plenty of people who devour meat three meals a day without giving it a second thought. You hear that it's bad for you, or at least excessive amounts of it can be, but that's true of everything, right?

Of course it's okay to eat meat, you think. Most people do.

Bringing a pig into the house hadn't been enough to make me want to shun animal meat overnight, like some vegan superhero turning his nose up at carnivores. (KaleMan: able to leap tall cornfields in a single bound!)

But realizing Esther had once literally been intended to be someone's dinner removed my ability to compartmentalize eating bacon while having a pig as a family member. Eating bacon now would be like eating one of our dogs. Or *any* dog. I started having little flashbacks in my head. I could see the dogs running around in the backyard and me rolling around playing with them, and then little Esther would run over to join in the fun.

Wait a minute, I thought, sitting by the kitchen. I glanced over at Derek and wondered whether the wheels were turning in his head too. He was looking at the meal he was cooking and down at Esther, back and forth. It was a heady scene. The little voices she was making, the smell in the air...specifically the smell of pig flesh being cooked. Right there in our kitchen.

I wouldn't eat dog. And I couldn't eat bacon anymore.

I didn't hesitate at all. I stepped into the kitchen, got Derek's attention.

"I don't think I can eat that," I said.

He asked me to repeat myself, so I did: "I can't eat that, I'm not eating that bacon, it's creeping me out."

His response surprised me: "I don't think I can either."

It was eerie. He didn't even question me. It was like he was thinking the exact same thing.

We still enjoyed our egg sandwiches. As I said, we weren't instant vegans. For the moment, at least, it was just: We can't eat "Esther." We carried on and ate our eggs and cheese, made a few jokes about how that wasn't the same as eating pig. We didn't know any cows or chickens, so they were just farm animals to us. There was no emotional connection with them. We had been researching pigs so much and learning how smart they were. Just by the way of the Internet, when you search for info on pigs, you obviously come across some not-so-pleasant info on how they're raised for food. That's where our love for Esther cemented the connection. When we looked at bacon, we saw Esther. But when we looked at a burger, we still saw a burger. All of a sudden Esther was on a different playing field, but our minds hadn't made the leap yet to her other farm "friends." It's a prime example of the disconnect and the walls we had built up.

Later that week, Derek and I were scrolling through the online Netflix menu when a documentary called

Vegucated caught our attention. It followed three content carnivores in New York who agreed to adopt a vegan diet for six weeks. We'd never intentionally gone looking for that type of documentary before—slaughter scenes are too graphic for me to take—but this one was described as light and comedic. I'd always been an "information" person. I loved documentaries of pretty much any kind. I was fascinated by films about engineering and history, and, of course I always enjoyed nature or animal films— unless they took place in Africa. No "circle of life" predator-and-prey stuff for me, thank you very much. Those things always end with a beautiful zebra getting tackled by a lion, and even though it was nature, I hated watching that.

When the option to watch *Vegucated* popped up on our TV, all I was thinking was that it looked like something worth checking out. Derek wasn't even paying attention to what I was picking, which was typical. He had his nose in his phone to read emails. So I just hit the start button and away it went. But when Derek realized this wasn't one of the usual documentaries I enjoyed, films on building the Airbus A380 or how wind turbines were built in the North Sea off the Netherlands—stuff he didn't much care about—his interest was piqued. He put his phone down and started paying attention.

By the end of that film, we had both begun to rethink our meat-eating lifestyle. From there, we watched other documentaries. *Food, Inc.* was about corporate farming in America. *Blackfish* investigated the lives of captive killer whales. We learned so much about where our food comes from, how animals are treated. There were so many cruelties, even in the things we used to think were okay.

I'd always thought I was a huge animal lover. But suddenly I felt very misled. I was angry about what we'd been told, how we'd been made to believe "they're just farm animals." I guess the information had always been there if we'd wanted to go looking for it. But we hadn't. It was too easy to just accept it and enjoy our carnivorous lifestyle.

So that was it. Simple as that. No more meat for me. It was time to go full-on vegan, to put my carnivorous lifestyle behind me and learn to love the produce section.

Okay, that's not true at all. Actually, as much as I wanted to stop eating meat from an ethical standpoint, there was one big obstacle in the way:

I'd always hated vegetables.

To be honest, I still do.

I could sniff out a sliver of onion in something and would pick around to get rid of it. God forbid if I got one in my mouth and crunched it, the meal was over. I was the simplest of simple eaters. Take me to a fancy restaurant and it's wasted on me—I want a burger or the pasta. Sometimes I would actually eat at home before going to a restaurant, because I knew I probably wouldn't like what was offered. Better to fill up before going out.

Derek asked me whether I thought we should go vegan, and of course I hemmed and hawed. As a tried-and-true veggie hater, I had a lot of trouble wrapping my head around the idea. I like what I like. I was afraid of having to eat things I didn't like, or even worse, foods I had never tried before. It would all be new, and new food is scary. A lot of what you hear about vegan food was scary to me too: couscous this and quinoa that. What the hell is quinoa and why would I want to eat it? Acai? I wouldn't even attempt to pronounce it!

I knew I didn't want to eat animals and was finally accepting the fact that chickens and cows really weren't all that different from dogs and cats (or pigs, obviously, who also stood on the "pet pedestal" we had built). But now I had this chilling question bouncing around in my head: If I can't eat meat, what will I eat? I hate salad. I hate weird vegetables, which to me is most of them. What was left? Was I going to be stuck with seeds and nuts? Would Derek come home one day to find I had morphed into a bird?

But I didn't say this to Derek. I eventually just said sure, we could do it. I didn't want to be the one to stop us from evolving.

So I made some small steps: I shifted my diet away from

meat. It was no longer the bread and butter of my diet, if you will. (Come to think of it, without meat, I ended up eating a lot more bread and butter.) But I'd still have a burger here and there. Milk was also hard for me to give up. I always tried to find a way to make it okay, and I was pretty good at convincing myself of things. I always had been.

But deep down, I knew I was trying to justify it to myself. The harder I worked to keep the blinders on, the more things kept sneaking into my line of vision. I would let myself get sucked in by industry marketing words like *free range* and *grass fed*. I'd think, *Oh well, if it's a happy cow, it's okay to eat it*, or *Those chickens lived in beautiful rolling green pastures and had awesome lives, so I can eat them now.*

And then there was my one big crutch, the one I held on to for months: *They don't hurt the cow when they milk her.*

Oh my God, was I wrong.

I'd always pictured milking a cow as happening on some beautiful farm on a lovely green pasture among rolling hills. Some sweet little Dutch girl with pigtails heads out with a bucket to milk ol' Bessie. Poor ol' Bessie probably wants to be milked. She's happy to provide milk for the family, and they love her for it. That's the story of milk, right?

Once again, a little bit of learning goes a long way.

From watching videos, I learned that cows on modern dairy farms are treated abhorrently. I started to find myself making comparisons I had never made before. I learned that human beings are the only species that drinks milk after infancy. We're also the only species that drinks another species' milk. That's a bizarre thing to do. You hear jokes about how weird it must have been the first time somebody decided to milk a cow...and then drink it? Forget the guy—what about the cow? What do you think she was thinking? She was probably like, *Uh...excuse me, but what are you doing?*

Early in our vegan transition period, for lack of a better term, Derek and I would go to a party and eat whatever was there. We had our supposed justifications.

I didn't buy it.

It's here anyway.

It's going to go to waste.

It's already prepared.

It took me a few months to realize that regardless of who buys the meat, there's nothing okay about it—at least not to me. As I got to know Esther better, as our bond grew, I couldn't help but compare her to a cow—or any animal bred to be food.

Where would Esther be if not here with us? In a gestation crate. I'd wonder what had happened to the rest of her litter. How do I know that pack of bacon in the store isn't a member of Esther's family? As far as I know, that could be her sister's litter. And even if it's not, it's still the flesh of slaughtered pigs. Pigs with intelligence and personality and affection and love—just like Esther.

When Esther first arrived she was a novelty, but as time went on and we started to learn a little more about the food industry, Esther became a trigger for the awful images we had seen online and in films we watched. As I watched her play outside, my mind would flip to the image of a baby dairy cow chained to a veal crate. I'd make her dinner and watch her loving every bite of her watermelon or mango and then find myself picturing a sad and broken pig in a gestation crate. I was feeling like a proud papa watching her reach these milestones of using her litter box and playing with toys, developing her larger-than-life personality, and then I'd be in the meat aisle at the grocery store, feeling physically ill because suddenly everything in there had a face. I couldn't see a steak or a slab of bacon as nothing more than a product anymore. Any one of those pork chops could've been Esther, and that was so upsetting.

The more time we spent with Esther and watched her character come to life, the more we realized that this whole "they're just farm animals" notion was bullshit. She had every ounce of the character and personality you'd find in any dog. There was so much more to her than I could've imagined, and every day she did something else to show us (even though some of it was super maddening, like opening cupboards and stealing food). Her heightened intelligence was key to our making the changes we did. *If she's this smart*, we figured, *every pig is.*

What's funny is that even once we know all this stuff, it doesn't always sink in. It's just like smoking: You know it's incredibly bad for you. You know you're killing yourself with every cigarette. But you keep doing it. People contrive reasons not to stop smoking even when they know they should. They continue until they finally land on a reason that truly matters to them.

Esther gave us the reason to search out the truth, to completely revamp our behavior—and to stick to it.

I'm not saying that going vegan is immediately the easiest thing you'll ever do. There's a learning curve, and it can be annoying. Grocery shopping takes longer at first. Looking at labels takes longer. People will make excuses like *I don't have time* or *It's too hard*. But honestly, it's *not* that hard. You just have to reteach yourself things you've been taught your entire life.

And if you want to make a difference, to my mind, you have to give up *all of it*. No meat, no animal products. (And you know how hard that is for me to say.) Derek and I knew we could never eat animals again, and we knew we wanted to make a difference.

Once we made the decision to *truly* go vegan, the

process was pretty interesting at first. We'd go grocery shopping and think we had done really well, only to find out our favorite brand of Doritos had milk in them, or that some other weird chemical-sounding name was actually made from cow tendons or something crazy like that. Giving up meat was relatively easy compared to learning just how many other things contain animal products. That's what really messes with a new vegan. I can't even tell you how many times one of us brought something home from the store only for the other one to notice something on the ingredient list that was *verboten* for our new lifestyle. Grocery shopping had been annoying enough back when we ate meat, but shopping vegan turned a one-hour trip into a three-hour marathon. We would spend forever standing in the aisles with two seemingly identical items, trying to figure out if they were vegan or not.

And while this dietary change was taking place, Esther was growing . . . and growing . . . and growing. Housetraining was proving to be a little more difficult than we'd anticipated, and even more stressful days were on the horizon. Specifically in the form of a prodigious amount of piggy pee and poop.

We had been told litter training was really easy. *You just show her a couple of times and that's it.* We first used a cat litter box with pee pads in it. (We couldn't use kitty litter because pigs will eat it, so we were told to use pee pads or wood shavings.) We bought the largest litter box we could find with a dome over it. Obviously, the plan was for her to go inside, do her business, and come out.

The first part worked out fine: She had no problem getting inside, but then things got tricky. Because of how the entrance was shaped and how *Esther* was shaped, she couldn't turn around when she got inside. When she peed, the stream would go...right out of the box. She was doing the right thing, just not having the right result. So we got a box that was two feet bigger and had to train her to go inside, turn around, and then squat and do her business. That proved to be exceptionally difficult. And as she got bigger, so did the litter pan. I'm talking a pan the size of a couch; if you can imagine building a box around a couch, that's how big her "bathroom" was. (If you've ever lived downtown in a big city, you've probably had a smaller bathroom, sink and shower included.) And each time we made the box larger, we had to retrain her. We'd lead her in, she'd turn around and do her business. We lined the inside of the cage with old plastic real estate signs, and the base was a baleful of wood chips.

As you can imagine, this was a nightmare to clean. And because the structure had a top on it, you couldn't just stand back and clean it with our version of a litter pan scoop. (You guessed it: a full-size shovel.) No, you had to climb *right on in there*. It was pretty labor intensive—and let's be honest, pretty gross—and we had to clean it no less often than every couple of days.

At that time, I guess because she still was growing, she drank *way* more water than she does these days. In one visit to the water bowl, she'd drink about *three gallons* of water. (That alone tells you how big a bowl we needed.) Of course, her bathroom habits weren't exactly perfect during those learning stages, and three gallons of anything is a lot when it's coming out where you don't want it. We tried to recognize her needs and have the box available when she needed it, but we were all learning then. Accidents happened, just on an exponentially grander scale than if you were housetraining a kitten or puppy. It was more like housetraining an NFL lineman. Possibly two.

When Esther's bathroom spot—you couldn't even really call it a box at this point, more like a port-a-potty—reached its maximum size, we moved it down to the unfinished basement, and that's where it stayed. We created a playpen area there for when we had to go out, because we couldn't trust Esther to be upstairs alone.

Problem solved, right?

Not exactly.

Even with Esther as contained as possible, with all of our improvised engineering and attention to as many details as we could fathom, there were more accidents.

The cleanup was a Herculean task: backbreaking, dirty work. Afterward, we'd think we were in the clear for a few precious moments. We'd spend an hour down there, take the cage apart, sanitize everything, remove the pan, mop everything up, and enclose all the waste in garbage bags. We'd be covered in mess, of course, having been down on our hands and knees cleaning and disinfecting. But at least everything else would be pee- and poop-free for the moment.

So we'd get changed and exhale and sit down to rest, and five minutes later Esther would come down and miss the mark by *this much*, and once again there would be a ton of backflow under the crate. And we'd have to start all over again.

We'd try not to lose our cool. As I've mentioned, in the beginning Derek put most of the cleaning on me, and it wasn't like I could argue the point because I'd brought Esther into the family without consulting him. But in time, to my great appreciation, he stepped up and shared the brunt of the work with me.

As she learned, Esther's bathroom habits improved substantially, but she still wasn't batting a thousand. No matter how well trained we thought she was, every so often she'd wander into the living room, squat right in front of us, and . . . release a flood.

We'd immediately start screaming "No!" in an instinctive reaction that often made things worse. Esther would realize she'd done something wrong, clench it off as best she could and start racing away, pee spraying out as she ran from one end of the house to the other. And away we'd go with the rug shampooer running, washing machine churning, tempers flaring. We'd put Esther downstairs in her pen because she'd been "bad" and that was how we reprimanded her, and hard as it might be to believe, that wouldn't even be the end of it.

Because Esther would just start *screaming*.

When Esther screams, she sounds like a jetliner. It's just wide-open wailing.

Honestly, it's heartbreaking. I'd sit in the living room and try to carry on with whatever I was doing, but I'd hear her cries, which—let's be real—were impossible to ignore, and I'd want nothing more than to let her out and tell her it was all okay. It's like that phrase *puppy dog eyes*, where a dog gives you that look that just gets you in your gut, or, of course, a crying baby: All you want to do is comfort them. I knew good parents sometimes (probably often) needed to tell their kids how to behave, that we had to discipline her or we could end up with a terror on our hands. I just hated seeing and hearing her so upset. It sounds so cliché, but I needed to be strong.

At the same time, a part of me worried that this would be too much for Derek to deal with. I knew Derek loved Esther by now, but in the back of my mind, no matter how remote I considered the possibility, I always felt there was a chance he would just throw his hands in the air one day and say, "This isn't going to work." I was still afraid I'd have to get rid of her if I couldn't get her behavior under control.

So I knew I had to get tougher. We would have to enforce some stronger discipline with Esther. It wouldn't be easy. She'd be miserable and we'd be miserable, because we knew she didn't mean to do anything wrong. But we also knew we had to reprimand her in some way.

We set her punishment: a half-hour timeout. We'd set the timer on the stove, endure thirty minutes of the jetliner, and then let her out. It was not uncommon for her to forget why she was put down there in the first place. (This seems to be common among all sorts of pets, but what can you do?) We know this about Esther because she would finally come out after her dramatic half-hour, come upstairs, and immediately do the exact same thing *again*. And then go right back down for another thirty minutes.

And that was her training.

We had a tough time with it. It went on for weeks, and as with any teaching/learning experience, it was often two steps forward, one step back. Or one step forward, five steps back. One day it would seem like we were making amazing progress, only to have a major backslide the very next day. I couldn't get the pattern down. Was it something I was doing wrong? *We were so good yesterday, now what fresh hell is this?* I'd think.

And of course there were other challenges. Just when I thought I had Esther figured out, she would outgrow the litter box or eat something of Derek's that she shouldn't have, which of course would piss him off to no end. We lost an endless stream of phone cords and computer chargers—she took a real liking to wires, and it was growing tiresome (and expensive) very quickly. We knew she didn't want to be "bad"—she was just acting on instinct, much the way dogs and cats do when they tear up items in the home. But we had to get the message across that this wholesale damage couldn't continue.

So we dealt with it. And we disciplined. And she wailed. And we'd start each new day hoping timeouts would be kept to a minimum.

Right before Christmas, Derek and I decided to take our first trip together since we'd gotten Esther. We were going to the home of Derek's parents in Barry's Bay, a small town between Toronto and Ottawa. Leta, my trainer from the gym and a good friend of ours, often puppy-sat for mutual friends and was great with Esther. She said she'd be happy to watch Esther for us and that we shouldn't worry about a thing. We were only going for three days, and we knew Esther's bathroom would be bad, but of course we didn't expect Leta to clean it. We really needed some time away, so we agreed to let Leta watch the house.

This was the first time we'd felt anywhere near comfortable taking a vacation since we'd gotten Esther. I say "vacation" even though it was only three days because our life had become so full of responsibilities that this was a vacation to us—and a desperately needed one at that.

The four-and-a-half-hour drive to Barry's Bay was uneventful, as was the visit itself...at first. But at one point, Derek dropped a bombshell: He told me he thought we needed to get rid of Esther.

I couldn't say I was completely surprised after what we'd been through, but nevertheless, it was incredibly painful to hear. I told him it would be fine, that we'd figure it out. In reality, all I felt was a sick feeling deep in my gut. I understood where he was coming from, but it ruined the rest of the trip for me. I worried that as soon as we got back, Derek would be on me to cast out our not-so-little girl. And I couldn't even let my brain start to ponder about what that would mean for Esther.

The drive home wasn't exactly tense, but the Esther issue hung in the air. We didn't speak of it aloud, maybe afraid that would somehow jinx the peace, but we both worried about what we would find when we returned. I knew Esther could be a handful, but I had reasoned it out in my head the way you rationalize when you really want something like a couple of days away. *She's been so good lately. It's just a couple of days. What's the worst that can happen?* (Never ask that, by the way.)

At times leading up to that point, I'd try to let Esther have more freedom. While Derek was gone, I'd leave her out of her crate and then leave the house to do some errands. I'd make sure to get home before Derek, hoping I'd later have the opportunity to tell him how good she'd been while we were out, but it virtually never worked out that way. Each of these little experiments ended with me frantically trying to clean something up before Derek got home to see it. My stress always came from trying to keep Derek from knowing about something she had done. I needed to justify all the "I can do it, don't worry, she'll be awesome" lines I'd fed him at the very beginning. And I meant it when I'd said it. I just had no idea what the hell I was promising.

On the drive home, my heart was in my throat the whole way. I was hoping for the best—not just for our sanity and the pleasant fantasy of coming back to a perfectly kept home with zero problems reported, but because I was nervous about what Derek would do if this little experiment was a bust. He'd opened the door to getting rid of Esther, and I didn't want anything to push her through it. I wanted nothing more than to walk in the house and find both a happy Esther and a happy sitter playing together in a perfectly kept living room. Maybe Esther in an apron, having learned to cook during our time away, just putting the finishing touches on a welcome-home dinner.

And then we got home and reality set in.

The term that comes to mind is *rock bottom*.

The house was a pit. Litter box shavings were spread *everywhere*. Every inch of the house smelled like urine. Scratch that: not smelled, more like *reeked*, like with an unbelievable, make-your-eyes-water stink. It was a disaster.

I felt sick to my stomach. I knew how badly this would play with Derek. The outcome wouldn't be good.

I'd already secretly been having these moments where I'd question everything: *Are we going to keep her? Did we do the right thing? How big is she going to get? She's ruining the house. She's ruining our life. She's ruining our relationship.*

Now, here we were.

This would also probably be a good time to mention that Derek has always been a super clean person—as in bordering on OCD. A bit of untidiness bothers him. A mess gets under his skin. A huge mess is practically more than he can handle.

And this was a mess like none other.

This was such a mind-blowing departure from what

our house (and our life) had been. I could see he was on the verge of tears, which crushed me. He didn't seem mad, exactly, but clearly he was hugely disappointed. And of course I was beside myself. I was partly upset because I'd let the house get so bad in such a short amount of time, but I was also embarrassed because now our house sitter knew exactly how bad it was and what we had to deal with. After shooting me an uncomfortable glance, she left us alone.

I had done a fairly good job of hiding messes from Derek, but there was no hiding this.

Derek and I walked around the house to survey the damage while Esther tagged along at our feet, no idea how close she was to being exiled. Her smile beamed, and she was full of joyful energy and curiosity, just as always. But for the first time I looked at her with uncertainty about what to do. I felt I was failing miserably, and she would be the one to suffer if I didn't make it right, and fast.

Neither Derek nor I wanted our house to be a place where you'd walk in and get hit with a brutal wave of stinky animal smells, of course, but for Derek to walk into this after we'd come so far was just too much. Even for me—you know, as a real estate agent you deal with a lot of smelly houses—you never think *your* house will be the smelly house. I'm the guy who leaves a place and says, "You wouldn't believe the shithole I was just in." Now my home was the shithole, and not just figuratively.

I didn't think I could be more mortified.

Then I went downstairs.

We'd been gone only three days. Urine was puddled on the floor, shavings were everywhere, and because the basement was unfinished, the urine had soaked into the porous wood and completely permeated the entire place.

Derek grabbed some cleaning supplies and got down on his hands and knees in her pen. Everything he touched or moved was covered in urine. Her bed, her litter box, her toys, and now Derek. He had rolls of paper towels and cans of Lysol and deodorizer all around. As he would pick up paper towels to put them in a garbage bag, they would just drip everywhere. It was so gross. He had a mortified look on his face. I had no words, because no words could make this better. There was no simple *I'm sorry* for this.

I think we were both thinking what neither of us really wanted to admit: She had beaten us. In my heart I knew this couldn't continue, and I know Derek felt the same, but he also knew how I felt about Esther and how upset I would be. I think he was hoping I would come to the decision myself. I'm sure if I'd gone ahead and been the one to say enough is enough, to make the call to get rid of Esther, Derek would have swiftly agreed.

It was a somber experience. I kept going upstairs to check on Esther while Derek stayed in the basement. I looked at her, wishing she and I could just talk like people, wishing I could explain how she was on the way to peeing and pooping and rutting and wrecking her way out of our home—*her* home.

I tried sending her brainwaves—when you're desperate, you'll resort to anything—to let her know this was getting dire and she needed to clean up her act.

During one of these trips upstairs, I had my first meltdown. I was looking at Esther, but my mind was on Derek. The man I loved was in the basement, up to his elbows in her urine, and it really was all my fault. I sat down at the top of the stairs, looking out at the backyard, and I just starting sobbing. I felt completely hopeless and broken.

Leading up to this, I'd had many moments of secretly crying when Derek wasn't around. Because I'd taken on the brunt of the cleanup chores in the early days, there were times I totally lost it. I'd tried to keep a brave face because I didn't want Derek to see me freaking out.

I was terrified that if Derek saw me feeling so overwhelmed, that would be reason enough for him to say she had to go. And I couldn't lose her. The thought of losing Esther was unbearable.

I kept going upstairs and down for about an hour while we cleaned her pen. When it was done, we went upstairs and sat on the couch. Neither of us said anything. I was too scared to speak, too scared to give an opening to what was surely going to come next. But then

Derek turned to me, and I could see it in his eyes: the genuine fear of broaching the subject we both knew had to be tackled, the sadness of someone who now loved her as much as I did.

"What are we going to do?" he asked.

As soon it was out there, we both started to sob. Things had been escalating for so long. We'd both been hiding how we felt about it. I wasn't the only one who'd been crying in private somewhere; now I found out he had been too. But in that moment, we came to a conclusion: *We have to get rid of her.*

I curled up in a ball on the floor, bawling like a baby. Shelby came over and lay next to me, and one of the cats climbed on top of me. Derek joined me on the floor, both of us crying, with all the animals crowded around us.

I don't know how long we were there.

I just know it felt like someone was dying.

Here's the funny part—not funny ha-ha, obviously, but funny unexpected: That point, that lowest of lows, was exactly what inspired us to keep Esther. The destruction she left in her wake made us miserable, certainly. It just couldn't go on like this. But that was nothing compared to the thought of actually getting rid of her. *That* idea was devastating. As bad as it had been, we needed to find a way to work it out, because we knew we just couldn't live without her.

So we needed to find a way—some way, somehow—to live *with* her.

We were going to fix this or die trying.

Thus the new housetraining plan. We got rid of the litter box and decided to take Esther outside every twenty minutes. Even if Esther didn't have to go. It didn't matter. Twenty minutes on the clock? Esther goes out.

And yes, I know that sounds like an insanely inconvenient solution, and you're damn right it was. But like I said, we were going to fix this or die trying. Even if the smart money looked for a while to be on the "die trying" side.

We started rewarding her with a treat whenever she peed outside. And she tried to help us help her. She'd go to the door and let us know that she had to go. Of course, we'd reward her if she did her business. But even if she didn't have to go, we'd still take her out at that twenty-minute mark.

But then she got smart and started to play us: *If I go out and squat and pee, I get a little treat.* So twenty minutes started to become ten minutes—she'd go outside and pee just a tiny bit, making sure not to let all the guns fire at once, if you catch my drift. She could milk it and get yummy snacks every ten minutes if she played her cards right. And we went along with it for a while, because she was doing her business outside and that was the ultimate goal.

Then she got cocky.

She'd go to the door and wail like she had to pee. We'd take her outside, she'd squat and *pretend to pee*, and then she'd look up at us, pleased with herself and expecting her reward. (She's always been very smart.) Most of the time we just laughed in her face because it was so funny, but it was also frustrating. Especially if it's three in the morning and Esther has a hankering for a cookie, so she wakes you up and you go outside for a garden tour in your underwear, only to realize she's doing a fake-out. So we stopped the reward plan entirely and ultimately, thankfully, she got the hang of it.

CHAPTER FOUR

I know it sounds like the perfect gay stereotype, but Derek and I always took a lot of pride in our home. It was by no means a mansion, but we kept it very neat. (Okay, *Derek* kept it very neat.) We decorated with a fun and funky style, we kept our gardens maintained impeccably, and we had the nicest lawn on the street (although my neighbor Rolph would—wrongly—argue that point with me). We lived in a manner that ensured that, should anyone stop by unannounced, our home was in presentable-enough shape that we wouldn't be scrambling to tidy up. The house was always ready for entertaining, and we *loved* to entertain. We had a very active social life, and the small menagerie we had assembled prior to Esther's arrival had an established routine, so we were used to being able to come and go as we pleased.

But as Esther grew, it became exceedingly clear that things would have to change. We had to learn along with her what she could get into and how we'd need to adjust things. And by "things" I mean the entire layout of the house. One day a lamp would go flying off an end table, and it would be clear that there wasn't room for a lamp (or an end table) there, because Esther needed that space to turn around. We basically "redecorated" as we went along based on how large she was at that time and thus what she could knock over. And it was fine; change is good. We'd never been really attached to "stuff," so having to rearrange didn't bother us. It was just a "learn as we go" process that kept repeating itself. Every time we thought we'd found a workable layout, Esther would find a way to prove us completely wrong. Eventually, we realized it wasn't about a lamp here or an end table there: We needed to completely Esther-proof the house.

That moment of clarity occurred the day I decided, in all my wisdom, to leave Esther alone when I went shopping. It wasn't to be a lengthy excursion—just a quick hop down the road to grab a few things at the grocery store. I'd been home all day, and Esther had been behaving quite nicely. I'd been able to clean the house, do some work in the yard, and clear a lot off the "honey-do" list. And feeling entirely too good about myself (and Esther's apparent domesticity), I wanted to run out for a few things I'd need to make a nice dinner for Derek when he got home. That would be the cherry on top of the sundae that was my very well-executed day.

It was pure bravado on my part.

So I took my leap of faith and went shopping. I headed

back to the house feeling great. As I pulled into our driveway, Derek's car wasn't there, so I knew he hadn't returned from his outdoor magic shows that day. I turned the key and opened our front door, and what I would find soon thereafter made me think Derek must have been sneaking magic lessons to Esther when I wasn't looking. Because she was now a bona fide Houdini.

But this wasn't an immediate realization. In fact, I'm embarrassed to say that in the initial moments when I walked into the house, arms full of shopping bags, I took a minute to admire how clean and shiny I had made our house.

Then it hit me. That wasn't the magnificent sheen of an expertly cleaned home—it was oil. Vegetable oil. One hundred and twenty-eight ounces of Mazola Vegetable Plus! Cholesterol Free cooking oil. *Everywhere.*

I'm not sure how she did it, but Esther had found a way to get into the gigantic jug of vegetable oil—one of those huge ones, basically a vat with a handle—and the entire kitchen, hallway, and walls were covered in it. The walls were literally dripping oil. Our house looked like the vegetable version of the *Exxon Valdez* had passed through. The massive jug had been demolished, and she'd somehow splashed and spread the contents onto everything imaginable. There was evidence everywhere: This would be the easiest case in the history of *CSI*, especially because Esther—who had apparently fled the scene of the crime and gone on the lam—had made a point of rolling around in the stuff. The corners of the dining room and kitchen had clearly been slicked by her rubbing herself on them. What fun.

As I stood there dumbfounded, surveying the damage, my heart sank. We had been doing so well. We'd had such a good day. And then the ominous question popped into my head:

Where *was* Esther?

I dropped the groceries on the counter and followed the oil trail out of the kitchen, down the hallway and to the bedroom door. (Suffice it to say you don't need to be Sherlock Holmes to track down a suspect whose hooves are coated in oil.) Outside the door, I closed my eyes for a moment and thought to myself, *Please don't let her be on the bed, please don't let her be on the bed, please don't let her be on the bed.*

I opened the door.

You can probably guess where she was.

She'd put some real work into it too, having rolled around for a while to ensure every inch of the sheets was nice and oily. And she was sleeping. All greased up and shiny. Perfectly content with that sweet little smile on her face. And snoring. I could almost feel guilty for trying to wake her. Until I actually tried.

Pig wrestling is a thing. People, usually kids or young adults, enter a fenced-off mud pit and try to grab mud-slicked pigs, which proves to be challenging and, apparently, entertaining. Imagine that with oil in the place of mud. True, Esther was stationary in this situation—hell, she was still out cold, and snoring away to boot. But she is a very large lady, so my trying to grab and move an oil-covered Esther from the bed while standing on an oil-slicked floor was a comedy of errors.

It started with the look she gave me when I had the nerve to interrupt her beauty sleep. Then she didn't much appreciate my trying to roll her off the bed while my own feet were slipping out from under me. She grunted and went back to sleep.

And to be clear, we had the very definition of a "ticking clock" in this scenario, just like in movies where the heroes' quest is made all the more challenging because they're running out of time: Work fast before the asteroid hits the earth. Work fast before the bomb goes off. Work fast before the building collapses under our feet.

Work fast before *Derek gets home*.

It might not sound as dramatic as the other scenarios, but to me, it sure felt like a life-and-death situation. The house was a disaster, I hadn't even started dinner, and Derek was due home soon. And here was Esther, dreaming her piggy dreams, snoring away, completely oblivious to the damage she'd caused and the fact that every passing second made my anxiety shoot up like a magic beanstalk.

I attempted to move her more forcefully, leaning into her, trying to wedge my arms under and around her ample body. But then she decided we were playing a game. We genuinely started to wrestle. The writer George Bernard Shaw reportedly once said, "I learned long ago never to wrestle with a pig. You get dirty, and besides, the pig likes it." *Truer words were never spoken.*

There I was, wrestling with Esther, and in the middle of it all I just started to laugh at how ridiculous my life had become. I wasn't angry. She hadn't meant to do anything wrong. But I was literally trying to wrestle a giant, oil-covered pig off my bed, *in my bedroom.*

I finally got her off the bed and was racing around like a madman to clean the house before Derek walked in. We'd been doing so well; I didn't want Derek to know we'd had another setback. Besides, what were the odds this would happen again? I just needed to clean it up and pretend it never happened. I had to turn this from a crime scene into a photo shoot for *Better Homes and Gardens* before Derek reached the front door. It was *Risky Business* crossed with *Ferris Bueller's Day Off* crossed with . . . hell, *Godzilla.*

The kitchen was the first priority. Then the hallway, the walls, the bedroom. The sheets agitated in the washing machine while I cleaned the kitchen. I put a clean set of sheets on the bed and tidied up the house. I honestly amazed myself when I realized I'd done everything I had set out to do before Derek got home.

Well, except for one thing...I didn't actually have time to make the dinner. Which was the whole reason I'd gone out to begin with, thus leaving Esther alone and giving her the opportunity to submit her application as a Tropicana nightclub dancer circa 1975. But at least the house was clean.

Determining Esther's worst kitchen disaster would be a highly competitive contest, but the vegetable oil tsunami would certainly be a finalist.

Someone needed to be home all the time to make sure Esther was taken outside to pee. (Doggy doors are one thing, but a piggy door is an impracticality.) And the idea of having guests over changed entirely. We always had to plan in advance to deal with the daily effects of "Hurricane Esther" to the house. We ended up making a little checklist to review before anyone could come over, something to keep our guests and their possessions safe. We went from relaxing with friends and a glass of wine to a state of hypervigilance, lest Esther start exploring any stray bag, purse, or backpack that had the misfortune of being within her reach.

It was a lot to handle, but we took most of it in stride. As much as we realized that having a pig in the house was new for us, we also knew that *being* a pig in a house was new to Esther. And all the while, she was growing up and learning how to manage her new surroundings. And when I say manage, I mean manipulate. So we had to take a lot of extra precautions, especially pertaining to food.

The trash cans were attached to the cupboards with bungee cords so she couldn't knock them over. We tried baby gates. We had to tape the freezer shut (and still do to this day). Because she could open the stove and drawers with ease, we had to find other places to store things where she couldn't get at them. But there was always that moment when we'd close a cupboard and it wouldn't quite latch and we wouldn't realize it. But Esther sure did, and the next thing we knew there would be twenty-five dollars' worth of cereal dragged out onto the floor.

If she gets into the dry goods, whether it's oatmeal, snacks, you name it, whatever she has is now *hers*. You can't take anything away from her once she's taken possession of it. She's like a dog with a bone. A big, strong, clever, and *very* emotional dog with what she considers a hard-earned trophy in her mouth. This isn't something you want to interfere with. You just have to clean around her, because the minute Esther thinks you're going to take something away from her she panics. She'll take off, parading around the house with whatever it is in her mouth, accidentally shaking its contents out everywhere. There is no stopping her.

At first, the added anxiety for us was a lot to deal with. Not that anything Esther did in itself was all that terrible. A chair knocked over, drinks spilled on the floor—nothing too horrible in any single incident. But over time, the incidents added up.

I dealt with it a little better than Derek did. He had come from a home where everything was always immaculate. His parents had set very high standards, and he took a lot of pride in following their lead. The home was always tidy. Broken things were repaired quickly (and properly—no slapping on some duct tape just to get by). You could eat off the floors of that home. So for Derek, the change was a lot to deal with.

I think the biggest problem was that he never got a respite. With Esther in the house, there was almost always something going wrong. One day she'd surprise you and be a perfect angel, good as gold, and you'd think, *Wow, she's getting it!* And then bang: twenty-five kilograms of basmati rice gets flung wall to wall in the kitchen. For months afterward we'd still be finding grains of rice, kind of like Easter eggs. One day we'd be cleaning the house and would randomly find grains atop a picture frame (hanging on the wall!) from one of Esther's episodes weeks earlier. We tried to teach her how to live in a house. Our teaching methods could also be filed under "trial and error."

The truth is, we were being played the whole time. Esther is ridiculously intelligent and one hell of a manipulator. If you had to describe her in two words, you couldn't go wrong with *smart* . . . and *opportunistic*. People always say pigs are smarter than dogs or cats. The truth is, it goes way beyond that. When Esther realized that stealing food got her in trouble, she didn't *stop* stealing food. Instead, she devised a whole new method of larceny that made it easier for her to get away clean: She'd do it in *steps*. Esther's schemes were brilliant: International jewel thieves could learn something from Esther.

The first time we realized she was up to something, we were sitting in the living room watching TV. There's a little half wall between where we were sitting and the kitchen, so I couldn't see Esther, but I heard some rustling, so I peeked over to see what she was doing. I watched as she opened a cupboard, then turned around and walked out of the room. I was intrigued, so I sat and watched. A few minutes later, she went back into the kitchen, so I got up and walked around, being careful not to follow her but making sure I could get a glimpse of what she was up to. By the time I got to the kitchen, she had pulled out a basket of food, but she didn't take it with her—she was leaving the room as I entered. I figured she had seen me coming and escaped before being caught. I put the basket back in the cupboard, closed the door, and went back to my chair.

About ten minutes later, I heard a noise again. I looked over and sure enough, the cupboard was open, and Esther was leaving the room again. I called Derek over, and we both sat where we could see everything. Esther waited patiently, then came back into the kitchen, pulled out the very same basket, and left the room again—still empty-handed, or empty-hooved, or whatever.

Derek and I just looked at each other. What was she doing?

So we waited. After about fifteen minutes, Esther returned, as nonchalant as could be. She just ambled into the kitchen as though she didn't have a care in the world and then...*BOOM!* She snagged a bag of pasta from the basket, spun around, and hauled ass down the hallway.

Derek and I stared at each other in disbelief. Had our pig just executed a three-phase plot to steal some penne?

We'd had pets with us since the day we got together, but never anything like this. Dealing with Esther was not like training a dog—she was a far more intelligent creature with feelings and personality, an animal who actually *challenged* us at every turn. And as maddening as it was sometimes, she was proving to be an admirable opponent, one you had to respect.

She really plays every part to the hilt, the diva actress, chewing the scenery, playing to the cheap seats—our porcine version of Jessica Lange on *American Horror Story*. For example, she does this thing where she sucks the floor. It's her go-to habit when she has a mint in her mouth: She bows her head and presses her snout to the floor like it's attached by suction. During her elaborate food heists, she'll do this and just kind of hang around like nothing is going on. *La la la. I'm just a pig hanging out and definitely not getting into any trouble. Don't mind me.*

That's our baby. Huge pain in the ass at times, but we're constantly amazed by her genius. Which she usually exercises by being a huge pain in the ass. And despite the little headaches she would give us throughout the day, afterward she always came looking for a cuddle. That reinforced for me that no matter how annoying Esther's presence in our small home could be, she was still this adorable little piglet that loved nothing more that lying beside you and tucking her face under your arm while she slept. I *melt* when she does this. How can you not? She really is just a big baby who wants attention and affection. And when we thought about the alternate life she would have had without us, it really made us focus on giving her the best life we could and concentrate on the big picture and not the annoyances. Esther wasn't just another dog: She had been destined to become someone's dinner. All the little headaches were nothing compared with saving this incredible being, this member of our *family*, from that fate.

As we Esther-proofed the house, we learned what she could and couldn't get into with her little shovel-snout. (Answer: *There is almost nothing she can't get into.*)

Our formidable opponent also resurfaced when it came to her water bowl. In the battles we fought with Esther, this very nearly was our Waterloo. Esther enjoyed flipping the bowl over. It was quite large and thus could hold a whole lot of water. We're not sure what pleasure she derived from it; maybe she just did it because she *could*—kind of like dogs licking their privates. Whatever the case, over the bowl would go, making a huge mess.

At first, this didn't seem like such a big problem. If the bowl itself didn't contain too much water, she couldn't make too much of a mess, right? So we got a large watercooler that would release water into the bowl automatically when the water got low. Easy. We cross-tied bungee cords to fasten the cooler to the back of the cupboards. That worked until the bungee cords lost some of their elasticity, at which point Esther was able to work her snout under the cooler.

Yeah, you see where this is going.

It was quite a scene the day she flipped the entire cooler over. Noah wasn't prepared for a flood this size. Water gushed across the kitchen and living room floors, and dogs and cats jumped to higher ground on the couches. Then Reuben slinked his way into the bedroom, and Shelby looked traumatized. Esther lay down in the middle of it all, flopping around like it was the greatest day of her life. (To her, it probably was.)

Undaunted, we stepped up to the challenge. Or rather, Derek did—he's the handy one. He gets it from his dad. Derek decided to screw a water bowl into the wall. *Let her try to move that.* I still remember him standing there with his arms crossed, looking very pleased with himself, and then his look of absolute disbelief as Esther tore off the bolts and knocked the whole thing over. The next move was to try a very large and very shallow bowl, two-and-a-half feet wide and only three inches deep, something she couldn't possibly get any leverage to flip. By now, you can figure out how that turned out.

The only thing that stopped it—and to this day I can't tell you why—was putting a small amount of *juice* in her water bowl. Strange, right? We found this out one day when Esther wasn't feeling well. She was picking at her food for the first time ever. She was walking much more slowly and hanging her head low. She looked exactly how I *feel* when I'm sick. She was also making little grunts and huffs and was listless. She also had a look in her eyes and an expression on her face that I didn't recognize. This wasn't our happy girl. She looked "down." She wasn't much interested in exploring or going outside. All she did was slowly pace around the house making her little noises and standing still in strange places like she was lost and out of sorts.

During this illness, the biggest difference was with her drinking. She typically loved water (both to drink and to swim in), but when she stopped drinking altogether, it was clear Esther definitely wasn't herself. And I was beside myself. I desperately wanted to know what she was feeling so I could fix it. But just like with any other animal (or an infant, for that matter), when you can't communicate directly with the ill party, you feel helpless. What was wrong with our baby?

I called the vet immediately, just like any nervous parent feeling desperate for answers. The vet said that pigs are just as susceptible to things like the common cold as humans are, that Esther most likely just had a virus, so we should make sure she stayed hydrated. We'd read somewhere that if you think your pet pig might be dehydrated, put a splash of juice in the pig's water bowl. So we did, and sure enough, she drank it. Just as important, she *didn't* flip the bowl. We kept adding a little juice to the water, Esther kept drinking, and soon enough she'd flushed the virus out of her system.

Our little princess was happy and healthy again. I was relieved. I was jubilant.

And so we stopped putting the juice in her water.

And she *refused to drink it.*

That's not all. As you've already guessed, she went back to flipping the bowl over. Pour in some juice, she's a perfect little lady. Give her plain water? *Bitch, please.* Flipped bowl and a dirty look directed at her dads.

So now, we give her water with a little bit of juice. Everybody's happy. I don't know who's training whom here, but there you go. That's how we do things now.

Of course, every time we thought we had things figured out, we'd learn how wrong we were. For example: groceries on top of the stove. (Those of you with big dogs probably see this one coming.) We knew she could get into the lower cabinets, we knew the freezer (which was at the bottom of the unit) needed to be taped shut and that our best bet was to keep it empty, but we never thought (at least at first) that she could get to groceries all the way on top of the stove. You can imagine my surprise when I walked into the kitchen and found Esther with her front hooves on the stove, stretched out taller than I am, her nose buried in the bag. I shouted Esther's name at the top of my lungs, startling her.

This was one of those (many) times when we learned that a startled Esther is not a good thing. Because as she tried to extricate herself from the situation, she ended up *bringing the stove down with her.* I don't know what scared Esther more, my yelling or the crashing of the stove and all the groceries. But Esther hightailed it out of there and down the hall.

Pooped little piggy.

I'll be social at the party, but don't expect me to spend all night walking around in these heels.

Is dinner gonna be ready soon? I've been sitting here waiting since lunch.

I feel like I should warn you now... I had cabbage with dinner.

"If you change the way you look at things, the things you look at change."
—Wayne Dyer

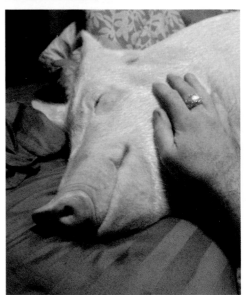

Family cuddles.

The day my
life changed
forever.

That better not
be kitty litter on
your nose.

I love you,
Grandma.

I know you brought home chocolate almond ice cream this afternoon, and I'm not leaving until I figure out where you put it.

That's for me, right?

Hand over the cupcakes and nobody gets hurt.

"The idea that some lives matter less is the root of all that is wrong with the world."
—Paul Farmer

The line forms behind me, everyone.

"When I saw you I fell in love, and you smiled because you knew."
—William Shakespeare

I'll always be Daddy's little girl.

I'm gonna take this stick inside—it's perfect for a wreath I saw on Pinterest that I have no intention of actually making.

Nobody gets in or out of this kitchen without paying the toll: Two cookies and a mango, please.

Oh great, first you get a pig, then you build a barn. I think we'd better move before the neighbors lose their minds.

I make my own bubbles in the bath.

If vodka in a Martini is made from potatoes, and they're garnished with olive...they're basically a salad, right?

But I don't wanna get out of bed yet.

Esther and Caprice close their eyes for a magical kiss.

"The people who are crazy enough to think they can change the world, are the ones who do." —Steve Jobs

The front of our stove remained broken. The freezer door was also broken, because she opened it thirty times a day. This is because there was a time when we *did* keep food in there, and Esther never forgets food. Memories of frozen edamame pods dance like sugarplums in her head. And as delightful as that memory might be to her, the way we remember it is this: Esther's teeth attached to one end of the bag, us holding on to the other, neither letting go until the bag split in half—and suddenly it was raining edamame. (*Hallelujah!*)

We've learned our lessons—sometimes more than once—but we ultimately learned that we can't keep *anything* she wants in the kitchen. And to the day we moved out of that home, we still had to make sure we'd secured our freezer with clear box tape, because she still tried to get in there. She was just like a human, the way we will look inside the refrigerator hoping to find something interesting to eat, even though we already looked in there an hour ago. It's as if we hope something new will magically appear.

Trying to keep up with Esther's calculating mind was a battle of wits. She was such a quick study that anytime we were somehow able to outsmart her, it seemed worthy of celebration. It was almost embarrassing: two grown men wanting to pop a champagne bottle for figuring out what kind of tape was most effective at keeping a pig from getting into the fridge. But she's so clever that it usually took several tries before something would work. It became like a game, and we were happy with any victories we could get. Because as insane as some (or all) of these adjustments may have been...she was our baby. When she nuzzles her face as close as she can get to you, just because she wants to connect and let you know *she loves you too*, there's nothing better. She was worth it all and then some.

CHAPTER FIVE

The holidays were approaching and by now Esther was well over four hundred pounds. Of course, the holidays are the time of year when everyone starts catching up—some people even still write those family newsletters. Newsflash: Everybody probably already knows everything you've done because they follow you on social media. But in Esther's case, even though people knew we had Esther, they didn't really know much about her, and they hadn't seen many pictures, because we were really trying to keep her private.

The reason for all this secrecy was that having a commercial pig was actually illegal where we live, because she's a hooved animal. There's a bylaw that says you're not allowed to have farm animals. A lot of towns have different laws about keeping animals, but the hooves are where you get yourself in trouble. Even potbellied pigs get you in trouble because of this hoof ban, so we kept Esther's presence really quiet.

When Amanda first asked me if I wanted Esther, I immediately checked all the rules and regulations, so I knew full well that we weren't allowed to have her. (By now, you've undoubtedly picked up on the fact that I'm the living embodiment of "It's better to beg forgiveness than ask permission.")

But I figured with Esther being so small—and because I was naïve enough to think she'd stay that way—we could sneak her past those silly rules without difficulty. And if it ever should come up, well, see that previous thing about begging forgiveness afterward. I'd just play innocent: Hooves, you say? Oh, you're kidding me! Pigs aren't allowed in our town? I had no idea!

I was planning to put up a wooden fence for privacy anyway and figured because we had two dogs, anyone who did catch a quick glimpse would assume Esther was just a puppy. A pink puppy. With a mushy little snout. Plus, we had a great relationship with most of our neighbors, so we didn't think they would be a problem either.

So in keeping with the "hush hush" of it all, only our really close friends and immediate family got to see Esther. For them, we thought, we would start a Facebook page exclusively about Esther. It would be a way for friends and family we didn't see often to keep up with her adventures, to see pictures and understand what it was like for us to be living with Esther. I suppose by *we*, I actually mean *me*, because (I hope you're sitting down) I didn't tell Derek I was doing it—I just created the Facebook page while he was getting ready to go out one night. It wasn't until we were in the car a little later that I told him I'd done it.

It seems funny to think about, making a dedicated Facebook page for a pig, but it was important to me to share with the people closest to us what our life had become with Esther. The first post was something totally generic. We hadn't found Esther's "voice" yet, so one of the pictures was of Esther indoors with a caption like, *What, you've never seen a pig in the house?* There was no direction; I didn't know what I was doing or that this was going to become a thing.

Here's how it actually went down. The night I launched the page, Derek and I were going to dinner at my aunt Erin and uncle Stu's house in Orangeville. It was December 4, 2013. While Derek was still getting dressed, I was messing around on Facebook, working on the page I'd built for my real estate business. I was familiar with the process of building pages and had the app on my phone, and I got the idea for Esther's page. So I sat on the couch and built it using the pictures I had on my phone.

Derek was ready to go before I was finished, so he

ended up waiting for me, standing over me and tapping his foot as I put the finishing touches on the bio. That first post consisted of two or three pictures, and I wasn't even thinking too much about what I was doing. I mean, who was going to see it? By the time Derek was standing at the door with his coat on, telling me we had to leave *now*, I just thought, *What the hell!* I selected a first post, pressed the Go Live button, and that was it. We flew out the door, now running a bit behind schedule for dinner, and raced to Orangeville.

We were just a few minutes into the drive, me at the wheel, when I told Derek to take out his phone. Usually, this isn't something I'd do, because if I'm driving and he's Facebooking, I feel like I'm just a chauffeur. But in this case, I had something exciting to show him. He looked confused, so I explained.

"Esther has her own Facebook page now."

His look went from confused to . . . more confused.

"Did she create it herself?" he asked, now understanding full well what I had been so preoccupied with before we left.

Derek pulled up the page. He read through the bio and immediately said he had a few things he wanted to add, so I made him an administrator. Well, I handed him my phone and told him to add himself, and then he just started playing with it. Throughout the ride, we kept seeing Likes and Comments, and Derek would read them aloud and we just laughed. We discussed the page settings and went back and forth between having Esther listed as a "pet" versus a "public figure," but we settled on "pet."

Little did we know what was to come.

By the time we got to Orangeville, the page had already gained close to one hundred followers. This was only a 45-minute drive. Where were these Likes and Comments coming from, and how was this happening so fast? By the time we finished dinner, I looked at the page, and it had over 150 Likes. This was all within a couple of hours. I got excited and thought, *Huh, that was really quick.* I showed the page to my uncle, because he was one of the people we had made the page for, and even he was wondering who those 150 people were.

My aunt and uncle are super fun. They both have the greatest sense of humor. Stu has the greatest stories ever, and my aunt Erin is always there, shaking her head and laughing along with the rest of us. Their sense of humor also meant they found it hilarious that we had been screwed and had a massive pig in our tiny house. To this day I jokingly tell them they are Esther's godparents.

I added another photo while we were at dinner and kept sneaking off by myself to see how many new Likes we had and what the Comments were. I immediately noticed many names I didn't recognize popping up, along with old friends I forgot I was even connected with. By the time we were leaving my uncle's house, the page had almost three hundred Likes. By the next morning, it had a thousand. The following day, it was two thousand. And the page just took off from there.

We didn't really understand what was happening or why. It turned out that a lot of our followers came within the first two or three days, mostly through a friend of mine who was part of Toronto Pig Save and who had shared our page. So our initial push came from the animal rights people, and we had a really strong vegan following, and then the general public just started finding out about us and falling in love with Esther. And so the page just skyrocketed.

Sounds great, right?

Well...

About ten days in, we started to panic. Esther's page now had more than six thousand followers. To me, having come from a small town and having run my small business page for three years on Facebook with only about 250 followers, six thousand people might as well be the entire world. And this could be a big problem. It was illegal to have Esther in our home, and with this giant following, we were worried that the wrong people would find out about Esther: specifically, zoning officials who would know that we were not supposed to be living with livestock.

(Okay, this might be the time when you wonder why I made the page public in the first place. Where were you when I needed you? Who am I, Mark Zuckerberg? You know I just forge ahead without thinking about consequences.)

I was also naïve enough to think that every single one of these thousands of people was from Georgetown and could potentially turn us in. I was convinced the whole town would show up and take Esther away in a van. (I've always had a vivid imagination.) So I contemplated pulling down the Facebook page. I made an appointment with a lawyer to find out just how deep a hole I had dug for us.

The lawyer confirmed that it was illegal for us to have Esther, but he also broke down the entire situation for us. He said it would take about eight months before anyone from the town could actually make us get rid of Esther. He said the first thing the town would do was fine us. We'd pay the fine, but we wouldn't get rid of Esther, of course. So then they'd fine us again. And then we'd go to court, and then we'd get tied up in court, and then ultimately it would end up in an order from the town telling us that we had to get rid of her.

So even though the end of that story wasn't necessarily good news—not that we had any reason to expect good news—it was good in the sense that we knew the town officials couldn't just show up out of the blue and take Esther away from us on the spot, which was what I'd been fearing since the Facebook page had taken off. If someone from the town did catch on and press us on the issue, it would be a long, drawn-out process. We'd know it was happening as it happened.

We also knew we had eight months to figure things out—and that was eight months starting from whenever we were contacted by the town, which hadn't happened yet. But we wanted to be prepared. Derek and I knew we most likely had to move anyway. Esther was still growing and we had no idea how big she would get, so we'd already decided to look for a small country property. This just put more of an official timeline on that plan.

Still, we knew this legal problem could cause us a world of hurt—we could face fees we absolutely couldn't afford, and we would have to fight a case we would ultimately lose. When we lost, we would either need to move anyway or give up Esther to stay where we were. (Obviously, I did not consider the latter an option.)

If we did need to move, that was another issue in itself. Where would we go that would allow us both to work but still be country property that we could afford and that would be suitable for Esther? Georgetown is a very expensive place to live, so a country property close to town in our budget would be in shambles or be a gas station or something else unspeakable like that.

Still, when we left the lawyer's office, we weighed the pros and cons and just decided to keep the Esther page going. Ultimately, we knew we would never give up Esther, and we knew we would have to find a proper place for us all to live anyway. It would happen sooner or later. Necessity is the mother of invention, and we were headed full-speed down the highway to necessity.

The page was growing at an astronomical rate. Thousands upon thousands of people were Liking the page and falling in love with Esther. We had not expected this at all. By the first week of January 2014, we had news crews coming by and the *Toronto Star* doing full-page stories on Esther. (So we obviously were leaning in to the whole media attention thing. At that point, we figured, *Hey, what the hell. Let's just do this thing.*)

All of a sudden (technically about forty-five days), we had thirty thousand followers, and we still didn't really understand why all this was happening. We didn't know why our story was such a big deal.

Even though Esther's page was immensely popular, when we thought about it, we realized it still didn't really have a voice or direction. It had amassed a strong following among vegans, so we decided to cater to them by giving the page a far greater pro-vegan angle. We started putting in vegan memes and talking about good plant product foods. But pretty soon after that, we started to see head-butting between the vegans and non-vegans. We'd never seen that coming, and we really didn't like it.

We've always disliked what we refer to as the Nazi-vegan movement, or, as they refer to themselves, Animal Rights: The Abolitionist Approach. This movement was started by people who I'm sure had good intentions, but they have black-and-white beliefs and harsh views of what constitutes a positive change. People who share those beliefs were constantly putting up posts on our page, criticizing us for what we were doing. They were even criticizing our followers for what *they* were doing. In essence, they were hijacking our page to push their agenda and alienating people who just wanted to follow our story.

For instance, there was a woman who posted a comment to our page that said, "I just want you to know that thanks to Esther, I've given up pork!" This was kind of a big deal to us. We had yet to understand what we would come to call The Esther Effect, and we considered that a win. A great step. And we told her as much. I replied, "Congratulations, that is a great step!" But that wasn't enough for the hard-core vegans. They tore into her for giving up *only* pork—and us for supporting her.

Now, let's be real. By that point, Derek and I were vegans, so of course we didn't want anyone to stop at just cutting out pork. Ideally, we wanted our followers to stop eating *all* animal products. But why chastise someone for taking a step in the right direction? I put myself in that person's position. If I wrote on a page to say, *Hey, I've changed my life in this way because of you guys*, and that person responded to me with, *Well, it's not enough; you should also be doing this and this and this*, I'd be like, *Well, screw you then!* And that would be the end of my connection.

So instead, we congratulated people on those baby steps. And then we'd get attacked for it. The Abolitionist movement would chime in on our congratulations and say things like, *How is this pro-vegan? Are you saying pigs are more important than chickens or cows?* Of course we weren't saying that. But they took a hard line and would post Comment after Comment that vegan was the only moral choice. That kind of negativity didn't foster what we were trying to accomplish.

We found ourselves in a mess as we were figuring out the page's direction and tone. A few crazy people attacked us for jokes they considered inappropriate. We posted a photo of Esther's giant rump and said, *Eat your heart out, Kim Kardashian!* We thought it was obvious that this was just a joke, but certain people jumped all over us—some claimed we were *sexualizing* Esther. I mean . . . really? It was ridiculous and honestly says more about the commenter than us, but we didn't want to do anything that would upset people, so we considered that in creating the tone of our page and decided to keep things mainstream and lighthearted. We tried to maintain that connection people were finding with Esther and to make them look for answers to questions on their own because they wanted to and not because we were ramming propaganda down their throats.

Every group has its own way of doing things. Take People for the Ethical Treatment of Animals (PETA), for example. That organization has hard-hitting, explicit print ads and very graphic, attention-getting street displays. That makes sense for PETA, and I understand why its leaders do it. We actually met with Ingrid Newkirk, the president and cofounder of PETA, and she told us exactly why they do the crazy campaigns. Here's the bottom line: Purchasing ads that would garner the same amount of attention would cost them thousands of dollars they don't have, so they keep the cash for situations where they can actually help animals. Instead of buying ads, they do outlandish campaigns. That's what they're known for.

Some people love it; others think the people behind

PETA are just a bunch of crazy extremists. But PETA is the largest animal rights organization in the world, and Ingrid's passion and commitment has inspired countless others to think twice before wearing leather or eating animals. She believes animals deserve the most basic rights—regardless of whether they are useful to humans. She spreads awareness that all animals are capable of suffering and have interests in living their own lives. Therefore, they are not ours to use—for food, clothing, entertainment, experimentation, or any other reason. Though you may disagree with some of PETA's outlandish methods, it's hard to disagree with the reasons why they do what they do.

Then you might look at Mercy for Animals (MFA), a completely different type of animal rights organization, with an entirely different approach—perhaps the exact opposite approach. MFA is a national nonprofit organization dedicated to preventing cruelty to farmed animals and promoting compassionate food choices and policies. MFA spends its time and money buying undetectable camera equipment, hiring undercover investigators, and exposing big agriculture for its horrible mistreatment of farm animals. This group's incredibly important investigations have shed light on the heartbreaking animal abuse that takes place behind closed doors. The investigations have led giant corporations such as Butterball, Tyson, Nestlé, and DiGiorno to drop products from abusive farms. That's huge. And MFA is totally different from the next organization. And the next one.

We've always felt like there was room for everyone, and it's not that we don't appreciate or respect all of the other groups and their very different methods—we don't begrudge anyone their place in the movement—we just felt that those types of organizations were very crowd-specific and put a lot of people off. With Esther, we had an opportunity to reach a *huge* spectrum of people with kindness and smiles and positivity.

This was a crucial moment for us. When we saw that we were alienating the people whose lives we could impact most—people like us who loved animals and wanted to do better but just hadn't made that connection—we knew we had to do it our way, simply with kindness and humor. We had no interest in the angry "You're not doing it right" approach. That sort of thing had played no part in our becoming vegan. We had come to our decision by getting to know Esther and asking questions and slowly understanding why going vegan was the better choice—ultimately the *only* choice for us. So we focused on kindness and humor and pulling heartstrings as opposed to harsh words and upsetting imagery, which I think is why the Esther movement is as successful as it is.

The Esther movement appeals to non-vegans in that it's all very approachable, nonconfrontational, and open, but it builds a connection to people. And we're finding that non-vegans love it because it opens their eyes and makes them think about things. Yet it still appeals to animal activists and existing vegans because we are a bright spot in an otherwise very sad and upsetting movement. We've actually had undercover investigators who are constantly reporting on abuse visit us because they want to be around a happy pig in a good environment. Esther was the morale boost they really needed.

As the Facebook page was taking off, we tried to respond to every single Comment, and we didn't have anybody helping us. Yes, we actually still try to respond to everyone. Can you imagine? (I guess that also falls under our abiding need to be people-pleasers.)

I was also noticing an influx of followers on my private accounts. Prior to Esther's arrival, my social media presence was mostly limited to my Instagram account, which had photos of me and Derek, along with the pets on occasion. It also had photos from our trips to Amsterdam and some things that might be considered a bit questionable by your average Esther fan. I mean, we were a couple of bachelors who liked to party now and then. We were just two normal, fun-loving guys who happened to have a pig. We hadn't lived the life of angels. We simply happened to have an awakening after we got Esther, and our lives drastically changed.

I came to realize that some people who wanted to follow Esther's story wanted to know more specifically about Derek and me. I could tell because when I went on Instagram, I found that strangers had suddenly started Liking photos I'd posted as far back as two years ago. Until then, I'd never thought my personal life would be of such interest. But for some reason, some people's fascination with Esther expanded into an interest in me and Derek. We weren't comfortable with it, so we ultimately decided to do a search-and-destroy mission for a lot of our online footprints. We'd become public figures of a fashion, and we realized it would be smart to say sayonara to material some people might consider a bit risqué. Shortly before Christmas, I converted my Instagram account to Esther's Instagram and removed all the personal stuff. We never would have thought Esther would take over all our social media, but the demand was there, so ultimately that became the best plan of action.

Our heads were spinning because of the unexpected impact our little Facebook page was having. It's been mind-boggling. In keeping our message non-preachy and mainstream, we've managed to spread awareness so far. We've been covered in *People* magazine's Pets of the

Week and also in PETA's magazine. Being able to have Esther make connections with people across such different platforms showed us that she was really striking a chord and that we could make a difference.

It was around then that we started thinking about recipes and creating Esther's Kitchen. And with that we lost all references to *vegan* and started calling everything "Esther Approved." Of course that means vegan, but so many negative connotations seem to come with that word that we decided to take a softer approach while still sending the same underlying message. And it worked! We didn't do this just because of the head-butting between vegans and non-vegans. We were getting a bunch of emails from non-vegan people who were telling us how much we'd opened their eyes about pigs. People from all over were sending us messages saying they had no idea how clean pigs were or how smart pigs were and basically retelling us *our* story. In reading these emails, we realized that Esther's photos and stories and funny captions had the same impact on other people as she'd had on us—and we were impacting people without having to "preach the message." I think our softer, non-confrontational approach, using humor and kindness and Esther's funny photos, was a big part of why Esther has been such a success in actually changing people's lives.

That's what we call The Esther Effect. Esther has had such a vast impact on people in so many different ways, we are constantly astounded. We met a French woman in Montreal who was in her seventies and already vegan. She introduced herself in very broken English. She told us how much she loved Esther and that she found Esther's page through one of her vegan friends. She said that Esther's page had actually taught her all the English she knew! She had started by translating the captions, and over time she needed to translate less and less. She was literally teaching herself English because of Esther, just because she wanted to follow Esther's story and know what we were saying—which was just incredible.

We also had a mother who wrote to us that she was a vegan and that she worked a lot in animal advocacy, but her husband and kids were meat-eaters. She said that she never wanted to force her opinion on her kids and had been very careful not to do so. But her son fell in love with Esther; he wanted to see what our pet pig was up to every day.

One day, the woman was looking at something on her computer about factory farms. Her son wandered over and saw the pictures of pigs in such awful situations and he started to cry. He asked, "Is that Esther?" She told him no, that was another pig, but it *could* have been Esther. She told us, "That was my opportunity to explain what was going on, because he was so fond of Esther and was confused by what he was seeing." That's when she explained to her son why she's vegan. She told us that the boy bawled his eyes out as he made the connection. He told his mom that as far as he was concerned, *all* pigs were Esther. On his own, he stopped eating meat. Even as months passed by, he was still vegan because of Esther. That blew my mind.

Life was busy, and we were trying to maintain our lives as we knew them before Esther. Derek was consistently booked for magic shows. I was doing my real estate work. When I had time, I was taking as many pictures of Esther as I could, to keep her Facebook page active. When we had downtime, we'd sit together in the living room, TV on, both of us facedown in our phones.

One night we were sitting in the living room, just doing our typical routine. Derek was reading messages and responding to Comments, and then all of a sudden, he burst into tears. I didn't notice at first. I was lost in my own stuff, not paying attention to him. But when I finally looked over, he was sobbing. I laughed at him because I knew he'd been overwhelmed and tense, so I thought he was just letting it all out. (I'm kind of a jackass like that.) But he didn't laugh with me as he normally would have. He was serious. He handed me the phone and told me to read it.

Derek had been reading a message to the page from a

woman who was vegan but her husband wasn't. They'd lived happily, each allowing the other to live and eat as they preferred for many years. But one day when they were in the grocery store together, her husband was ahead of where she was in the aisle. She watched as he picked up bacon and then put it back. She said nothing to him at the time, but when they got back in the car, she asked about it. He looked at her and just said one word: "Esther." And it was understood. He couldn't eat bacon anymore.

I felt a pit in my stomach when I read the message. It's hard to explain how it feels to read that kind of message. I had never been told by anyone that I had that kind of an impact on them. Clearly, neither had Derek. This was an older couple, dare I say, probably in the third act of their lives, and that someone of that age would even consider changing his life led to the realization of how powerful Esther was and what potential she had. And this was all without our saying things like, *You should be vegan* or *You shouldn't be eating this* or *You shouldn't be doing that*. A picture and a caption. That's all it was. They had such an incredible influence on people we'd never met or spoken with. How was this possible?

Photos of Esther making people laugh and smile were helping them make the connection on their own, without our pressing a negative message or showing horrific photos that most people ignored—ourselves included. Esther was a very real being who was having a very real impact. This was working out better than we ever could have dreamed.

CHAPTER SIX

When you think of Christmas, what comes to mind? Ornamented trees with twinkling lights? Kisses under the mistletoe? Beautifully wrapped presents? Christmas songs that started playing the day after Halloween without even giving a thought to poor Thanksgiving?

For us, it was all of that plus the complex logistical gymnastics of planning our family visits while making arrangements for the animals. We were days away from Christmas, and after our usual back-and-forth about how long we'd be away, the dates were set: We would visit Derek's family on Christmas Eve and come back the morning of Boxing Day (December 26) to see my mom. We'd lined up Leta to watch the pets and even miraculously got our shopping done in time. Everything was going according to plan.

Until it stopped.

And by "it," I mean *everything*. On December 21, three days before we planned to leave, an ice storm hit and took everything out. We lost our power, our heat—everything that makes life worth living, at least to my mind.

If you've never experienced an ice storm, it goes... well, the words *ice* and *storm* convey it fairly well, but the details are pretty juicy: Freezing rain coats everything. It's insanely cold, so you'd think it would snow, but it doesn't. It's this bone-chilling rain that otherwise seems harmless at first. It turns everything into icicles—a beautiful winter wonderland. Make that a beautiful, *dangerous* winter wonderland.

Imagine the worst blizzard you've ever seen. Now raise the temperature a few degrees to the point where instead of snow, it's just incredibly cold water. The water sticks to every surface, and when the icy air hits the water, it freezes. It's actually quite lovely... until you try to move. Your driveway becomes a skating rink (people literally skated down our street that day), the roof of your house creaks from the weight of the ice shifting, and your biggest fear after that is a sunny day. That's when things start to melt a little bit, and you don't know what's going to come crashing down around you.

We'd known there was a big storm coming. And as is often the case in these situations, some people were buying up all the water and canned goods at the grocery store. By contrast, we were there just picking up some watermelon for Esther. I know that sounds like a questionable decision, but we get storm warnings *all the time*! They rarely turn into anything major.

You hear the same thing from people who move to Florida or other places where hurricanes tend to come through. Yes, occasionally a hurricane actually endangers property and even lives. But most of the time, the hurricane just fizzles out over the water or diminishes to a tropical storm, and the only thing most people have to deal with is some heavy rain and wind. Something truly devastating, like Hurricane Katrina, is by far more the exception than the rule. Usually, it's much ado about nothing.

So we didn't pay much attention to this particular ice storm warning. Who can know when a bad one is really going to hit? Call it Boy Who Cried Wolf Syndrome. Or call it very bad planning. In my defense, I *couldn't* plan. Our lives had changed so much that I think I was in denial just as a defense mechanism. Before we had Esther, if we knew we were in trouble, we could pack our pictures and our dogs and cats, get into a car, and get out of Dodge. But now? Any emergency evacuation plans were out of the question. Fun fact: You can't pack a 500-pound pig in a car. And in the back of my head, I had this dreaded hypothetical where Derek was saying, *We need to leave!* and I was refusing. I'd be that guy on the news, clinging to his dog on the roof during a flood after everyone else had left. The helicopters would be flying overhead and people on Twitter would be tweeting *What a dumbass. ROTFL* and I'd just be up there like Tom Hanks in *Cast Away*. There was no way I would leave Esther behind in a cold, dark house with no idea when the power was coming back on—not even with a house sitter.

Just after the storm first hit, Derek and I went for a walk. The landscape was truly breathtaking: Everything looked like it was made of crystal. But then a tree cracked and fell. Out in the distance, there was a pop and a flash of incredible blue light. That was a power line going down . . . and our power going out with it.

In the morning after an ice storm, you can walk around and see the damage it did. This time, it was a disaster area. We didn't have access to broadcast television (we mostly just watched things on Netflix), so we hadn't seen any news coverage and didn't realize how bad the situation was. We woke up expecting the power to be back on, but it wasn't, and our place was *freezing*. At its coldest point, it was two degrees Fahrenheit. It was brutal. And *we* knew why it was so cold, that we had no control over the lack of heat inside, but our poor animals didn't understand. We had five sad, freezing faces looking up at us like, *What's going on? Can you turn the heat back on please?* We felt terrible. I remember looking at the dogs that morning, and I could see their breath.

Inside the house. (Dog breath smells bad enough in the first place. We don't actually need to *see* it.)

All things considered, the first night went okay. The following day was when it got bad. And by that night, it was complete chaos. Trees were falling—big trees—through people's houses. Ceilings caved in. When we stepped outside to get power from running our cars (we had to get it from somewhere), we could see the devastation around the community. It was terrifying. And of course, by necessity, every business was closed. It also continued to rain the entire second day. We could hear trees falling everywhere, smashing cars, dropping power lines. I'll admit it was pretty exciting in one sense, but it was also frightening.

The second night, we still had no power. It was tough enough on Derek and me, but we also felt guilty and helpless about the animals. They're our family—our *children*, in a very real way. Imagine how you'd feel knowing your children were suffering and there was terribly little you could do to help them.

This time we all slept together, huddled around Esther on the floor. We were quite the menagerie. One upside is that Esther is like a furnace—she's always radiating heat. (Imagine the body heat coming off an average-sized person and multiply that by four. And it's actually even higher, because a pig's typical body temperature ranges from about 101 to 104 degrees Fahrenheit.) Derek and I wrapped ourselves in our winter hats, gloves, and coats and swaddled Shelby and Reuben in the blankets, and we all snuggled up with Esther. The cats rested on top of us, using us for body heat, but not coming under the covers—I guess that notion was just a little too Kumbaya for those two. We survived the night and woke up to...no power. Still.

Meanwhile, it was getting dangerously close to Christmas—it was December 23, and Derek's mother was calling us every few hours to see when we were coming. We told her we'd keep her posted, but time passed and the power still didn't come back on, and things were just getting worse.

I didn't want to be the one to say it to Derek. He already knew there was likely no way we would make it to Christmas with his family. Still, we were packing up our things and planning to make the four-hour drive, even though our lives had become somewhat of a cross between *A Christmas Carol* and *All Creatures Great and Small*.

We did our best to function and create makeshift utilities while we figured out what we were going to do if this kept up. Our improvised stove was a bunch of tealight candles in a pot with a metal grate. We'd heat soup in a second pot atop the grate. We were literally cooking by candlelight, and as romantic as that sounds, it just plain sucked in practice. It took about an hour to heat a can of soup, so if you suddenly got hungry you were basically out of luck. (Unless you're really into cold condensed soup. I am *not* into cold condensed soup.) Everything had to be planned ahead, and it just got exhausting.

And let's face it: I'm a bitch when it comes to this stuff. I want my TV shows. I want my Internet. This is the twenty-first century. If we want something, we want it now. Thanks to gadgets, we *have* it now. And suddenly we were dependent on battery life for our devices. We used our cars to charge the phones and our candles to heat water and to "cook" to the best of our ability, but people were lining up for three hours at a Tim Hortons restaurant for a cup of coffee. The town was at a standstill. We took turns charging our phones and using tethering apps to provide online access to our computers. We still had to keep up with Esther's Facebook page, along with communicating with our families, but the novelty quickly wore off and the fear of disappointing Derek's mom (and thus Derek) was stressing me out most of all.

It's crazy how something so beautiful—outside our windows it looked like everything was coated in crystal—could be so destructive. It went from *Cool. We'll probably never see anything like this again* to *Fuck this ice storm, fuck my life, I am over this!* Whenever we got a glimpse outside, we would be reminded it was worse than we thought. The sturdy trees were bent over, begging for the ice to be gone. We finally realized we were going to be without power longer than we'd expected and that we needed a generator. Which would be fine, except the only generator available to us was $5,000—not something we could afford. We finally told Derek's parents we wouldn't be able to come and why. They were disappointed, of course, but they came up with their own plan: They'd come to us for Christmas. Even better: They'd bring a generator.

That must seem like a piece of really good news, and of course it was, but honestly, it didn't do much to lift our spirits. You could have told us we'd won the lottery and it would sound to us like we'd just gotten called for jury duty. By Christmas Eve, we were completely hating life. We had been without power for four days and wanted nothing to do with Christmas. We wanted nothing to do with the company of other people. We just wanted to wallow in our misery.

And right in the middle of this bitter cold, Esther went into heat.

Not that we knew what it was at first. It was her first heat. We hadn't ever dealt with her cycles before, and it took a while to realize she was having her period. And this would not bode well for the family visit. Derek and I already were stressed out and close to snapping. The other animals were freaked out over the disruption the ice storm had caused in the home. And Derek's mom was already *terrified* of Esther. Now add that Esther (understandably) was being a terrible bitch, and this was a recipe for disaster.

This is where I'd love to say that everything turned out fine regardless. That would be cool, right? Just like a movie. Everything's darkest before the dawn. Our scrappy team of also-rans is down three runs, it's two outs in the last inning, and the kid who struck out all season is at the plate. But then he hits a homer and wins the big game!

Nope, it didn't go like that. It was just as crappy as you would expect.

Derek's family arrived midday on Christmas Eve. It was Derek's parents (Brad and Janice), his sister, Nicole, and her boyfriend, Justin. Our place, of course, was a mess. It was dark and ice cold, we obviously hadn't planned on hosting Christmas, and we hadn't really cleaned up in four days. I just wanted to climb into a hole and die, but Derek and I tried to put on our happy faces. We did our best to act like we were thrilled to have four guests in our dark, Arctic home for a spontaneous party.

One upside to the sudden change of plans was that Brad and Janice got to actually see how bad it was. If they hadn't visited, they might have thought we were exaggerating just to get out of going to their place. Even they were shocked to see the devastation throughout our town.

In retrospect, we actually got pretty lucky in the storm damage department. Our only permanent loss was one tree. But at that time, we weren't feeling lucky at all. We felt like crap, and somehow we now had to prepare a Christmas meal. I was moody, Derek was stressed, and Esther was being nasty. (In fairness, she'd never had her period before, so it was probably scary for her in addition to everything else.)

And Janice, no shocker, was already freaking out.

It became clear almost immediately that Esther and Janice had as much chance of getting along as Bill Maher and Sean Hannity. Rosie O'Donnell and Elisabeth Hasselbeck. Paula Deen and a salad.

From the very first moment the family arrived, everything went to hell. (Well, even more to hell. It was pretty damn hellish before they got there.) Esther immediately got very pushy, not letting Janice stand anywhere. When Esther wants to get a point across, she uses her head, giving new meaning to the word *headstrong*. She uses her head to push you around, and that can be a problem for anyone, much less someone the size of Derek's mom.

Janice will tell you she's five feet tall, much like a five-foot-eleven man will tell you he's six feet and Steven Seagal will tell you he's a police officer. In reality, Janice is four eleven, which isn't demonstrably more vulnerable than five feet, but either way you're kinda screwed when a 500-pound pig decides to take issue with you. We're

used to Esther's size, but Janice is not used to contend-
ing with this type of thing. *This type of thing* specifically
meaning Esther continually banging her head into poor
Janice like they were at a Metallica concert.

This obviously did not endear Esther to Brad any more
than it did to Janice. He wanted to protect his wife, like
any good spouse would, so he was getting uneasy and
telling us to put Esther away. It wasn't helping the whole
"Brad and Janice hate Esther" narrative. I couldn't blame
Brad or Janice for feeling that way under the circumstances, but I'd so hoped things would go well. I'd hoped
they would come to see her the way Derek and I did: the
love, the loyalty, the companionship.

Unfortunately, all they could see was Esther being an
asshole. Mostly because she was being an asshole.

Esther is typically so sweet, but this situation was
anything but typical. She wasn't behaving at all. Derek's
family had only been there a few minutes, and in addition to the head-butting, Esther started parading up and
down the halls, *screeching* her displeasure. And Derek's
mom was running in the other direction, slamming
doors behind her.

Janice doesn't like to start off on the offensive. If she's
displeased with something, she'll usually make her point
known via another person (or several other people). Ideally, she builds a team of people with the same opinion she has before launching an attack. For example,

she told Derek's sister to let us know she was terrified and would appreciate it if we'd lock Esther up and not let her out until their visit was over. She had already complained to Derek several times since her arrival, and Derek hadn't responded the way she wanted, so she sent Nicole after us. There were also tears and arms flailing as she stood in the background and watched people do her bidding. And if something didn't immediately happen the way she wanted it to in this situation, it would escalate and get very dramatic. Trying to figure out how best to have Janice and Esther peacefully coexist in the same house resulted in a tearful *You love her more than me!* Janice is not what you'd call subtle, but few things are in our life.

We're pretty much immune to the sounds that come out of Esther. If it's just Derek and me in the house, it's no big deal. We *love* her. But with someone else, it's basically like putting up with a screaming baby. Specifically someone else's screaming baby. Because your own screaming baby pretty much doesn't bother you after a while. *Someone else*'s screaming baby is the Antichrist. And then when someone points out your baby's behavior, it makes you feel bad.

Look, it's not like I don't get it. Not everyone is equipped—emotionally and/or physically—to share space with a massive pig. It's a lot to handle, and we were asking Janice and Brad to accept conditions that would freak out lots of people. If you were visiting a home and kept being pushed around by a 500-pound animal, you'd probably want the creature (and it's certainly a creature, not a loved one, in your mind) to be locked up too. I can empathize with that perspective. They saw Esther in an entirely different light than we did.

But it still hurt, largely because I knew they already had massive concerns about Esther. They were always saying we should get rid of her and that pigs should be outside. They'd never known any different. As far as they were concerned, pigs were just food. To them, it made as much sense treating a cantaloupe as a pet as a pig. (More sense, really, because cantaloupes don't grow to several hundred pounds and go around head-butting people.)

I felt they still thought Derek was only going along with the whole Esther thing because I wanted him to. I knew that wasn't true and that Derek loved her too, but they remembered how upset he'd been at first when Esther showed up. That's what stuck in their minds. And again, I take responsibility for how that played out, but things had changed a lot since then.

Not that such things mattered much when Esther started ramming Janice around the house until Janice started to cry and literally locked herself in a bedroom. Again, the family had only been there for a few minutes. We hadn't had a chance to set up the generator yet and get the power on, so the whole scene was cold, dark, and ugly.

It's understandable to wonder whether we should have just put Esther outside when the family arrived. The problem was that outside really wasn't a place for an animal (or anyone) right then. It was slippery and freezing and dangerous for her.

Regardless, even I knew she *had* to go outside at that point, even if it was only while we dealt with the top priority of cranking up the generator. I played chaperone to Esther in the backyard so she wouldn't be alone. Derek and Brad dealt with the generator. The plan was to start by getting the furnace going (finally) and then get the refrigerator back up so the food wouldn't go bad.

Derek's dad is great at this kind of stuff. He's the one you want when the ship's going down. He has patience for days (a really important trait in this sort of situation), and he's also a great planner. He and Janice had planned this dinner since October. The dinner they were no longer hosting.

Not ten minutes after Derek and his dad began rewiring the sockets, the lights came back on! Finally, we had heat *and* light! Derek was pretty stoked, but then he realized that the whole town's electricity just happened to come back on at that moment. It had nothing to do with their handiwork. (Not that they wouldn't have gotten it working—it was just a funny fluke of timing.) Ultimately, no one at the time really cared *why* we had power, because *we finally had power!* We could live like human beings again. And if it sounds like there's no way I would have survived in the Middle Ages or any other era before electricity, you're damn right.

The fact that Derek's parents were no longer hosting did *not* mean they planned to alter the menu, which meant they were going to deep-fry a turkey. They didn't tend to be sensitive to things like us being vegan (or that the reason we *became* vegan was just outside, five feet from the deep fryer).

I walked past the kitchen and actually did a double-take when I saw Brad setting up the *deep fryer*, readying it to be taken outside. Esther was right there. In the backyard. Where they made me move her. This was twenty-six kinds of wrong.

"Brad," I said. "Really? Are you really doing this?"

Of course I could see that *yes, he was doing it*, but I was at an immediate loss for words. Then I looked at Esther. I was now moving past the fact that he was about to deep-fry an animal and working toward having it happen in the least offensive way possible.

"Can you at least move the fryer to the side of the house?" I asked. "Esther is right here."

He looked at Esther and then back to me. "And?"

He wasn't getting it. "Can you just move to the side of the house? There's actually a perfect place on the driveway where you can cook."

"It's just easier to do it here," he said. "You can see Janice is doing all the prep in the kitchen right there."

Yes. I could see that inside the door, up the stairs, and a few steps to the left, Janice was doing the prep. I knew the layout of my house. What I did not know was why moving just twenty feet was such an issue. Cooking the turkey by the side of the house would've meant having to walk out the front door, around the side, and up the driveway. That's a total of maybe thirty-five steps, easily accomplished in under a minute. But Brad wasn't having it.

Two minutes later, Nicole came to me as a full-fledged member of Team Deep-Fry. She said, "Dad really wants to cook the turkey out back."

Yes, I'm aware.

"The front stairs are really icy still."

She started to say something else, but I interrupted her.

"There's salt and a shovel," I said, pointing them out. "Right there. You know what gets rid of ice on stairs? Salt and a shovel. It's really easy."

Then Derek was suddenly standing behind me.

"Maybe we could put Esther downstairs so Dad can cook his turkey out here," Derek said. "He won't let it go."

"No!" I said. I'd already stuck her outside when I didn't want to, and now they wanted me to put her in the icebox basement? No way!

It felt like I was being pressured to do everything to

keep the Walters happy with no regard for myself or Esther. And I know it put Derek in an awkward position too. But our standstill didn't matter anyway. A few minutes later, I saw the side gate open and Brad come in with his fryer.

"It's too windy out there," he said.

I was livid. It clearly didn't matter *where* I wanted them to cook the turkey (not to mention *if*). It was happening at the back door and that was that. So in the spirit of just getting through this somehow, I relented.

I ended up putting Esther in the basement so they could fry their turkey in our backyard. Meanwhile Esther was completely out of sorts from being freezing for four days plus having her period, and now I was locking her in a cage? She was not happy. So I wasn't happy. I stayed with her as long as I could, but eventually I had to go upstairs.

They ate their turkey. Derek and I ate the sides. That's all Derek and I *could* do, because we hadn't planned on eating at home. No Tofurky or similar option for us. We kept the adult beverages topped up the whole time— out of necessity. Derek was unhappy. Derek's mom was unhappy. I was unhappy. Esther was unhappy. We knew Derek's parents didn't want to be there. But we soldiered on through dinner, and that didn't make ours so unlike other family Christmas dinners. With generation gaps and all the political and ideological differences these days, how many families actually *are* happy at their holiday meals?

We weren't mean to one another. No needling, no passive-aggressive criticisms under our breath. Derek and I were frustrated at the turkey scenario and essentially everything else, but I didn't want to rock the boat with his parents. I'm sure they felt terribly inconvenienced at having to come to us for Christmas and thus not being able to see Derek's grandparents and other relatives. They weren't necessarily thinking about how inconvenienced we'd been. It was an ordeal for everyone. We were just trying to stay lubricated enough to not go off the deep end.

We wound up opening presents on the floor that night. We had no tree, so it was the least festive Christmas gift exchange we'd ever had, but we did the best we could.

As we all sat on the floor, pretending this was the best day ever, Derek and I kept looking at each other, half smiling and thinking the same thing: *We're never doing this again.*

Meanwhile, poor Esther remained in the basement. Brad and Janice went to bed early. Derek, his sister, her boyfriend, and I ended up drinking another bottle of wine.

Our visitors left very early the next morning, undoubtedly relieved to be on their way. Derek and I were relieved as well, but it was definitely a Christmas we'll never forget. We have friends who never see their families for Christmas, and I used to wonder why they would do that. As the years tick by, it's becoming increasingly clear to me *exactly* why you would do that!

It was painfully obvious that we had outgrown our little house. Once the power was back on the visit should have been fairly straightforward, but with the close quarters it was a virtual debacle. Ice storm aside, our family had outgrown the house. Add company and it was just a recipe for disaster. We were starting to come to terms with the fact that we really needed to get out.

CHAPTER SEVEN

L et's face it, we all love a reason to celebrate. And aside from the requisite holidays, birthdays, and anniversaries, there aren't that many built-in excuses in life to do so. Okay, weddings, job promotions, and pregnancies probably should be in there too. And well... Fridays, meal times (yay, food!), and making a yellow light just before it turns red...

Okay, fine, I guess there are lots of reasons to celebrate—especially now that social media has deemed every single day some national holiday. (Pancake Day? Left-Handers Day? Really?) But that didn't stop Derek and me from also creating our own milestones to celebrate as Esther's fandom grew. (I've always been up-front about the fact that we like to party.)

Esther's page reached a hundred thousand Likes at the end of February, which is to say just eighty days after it launched, so we decided to commemorate this milestone in style. And by "in style," I mean we carved a watermelon with "100,000" in it and presented it to

Esther as a trophy. A trophy she could eat. As you can imagine, it was well received. When she chomped into it, watermelon squirted in all directions—*everywhere.* We did it indoors, and it was a spectacular mess: the ceiling, the cupboards... watermelon even sprayed into the other room.

And that's when someone from the *Toronto Star* reached out regarding doing a story about us. From the time we started the Facebook page that first week in December, we were just kind of going along with everything as it came. People would reach out to us and we'd respond, and it all felt safe because we were still communicating online. The virtual interaction gives you that arm's length feeling of safety.

But the *Star* was our local paper, and even at a time when the newspaper industry is steadily on the decline, it's still a huge deal. The *Star* is the largest daily newspaper in all of Canada, if you can imagine. It's been in business for more than 120 years and still maintains a weekday circulation of well over 350,000. (That would be huge even for a U.S. newspaper, and keep in mind that Canada has about one-tenth the population of the United States.)

So while we remained a bit worried about making Esther's illegal presence in our home *too* public (much as it might seem otherwise), we couldn't say no to the *Toronto Star.* As much as I go on about our concerns over the zoning laws and all that, I know it's obvious to anyone reading this that we were proud of our girl and wanted her to enjoy her moment in the spotlight! If it backfired on us, we figured, *So it goes.* Like I said before, we knew we'd have to move eventually anyway, and we knew we'd have time to make plans when the hammer came down. Even if we didn't exactly know what those plans would entail.

We hoped to achieve something else from the article. We wanted the wider audience the newspaper could reach to share our personal transformation because of Esther. We wanted them to see her smile and make the connection that this wonderful animal was their bacon. We also wanted to make it clear that people shouldn't run out and get their own pigs just because they fell in love with Esther. This was a drastic, life-altering situation for us. Though we'd found a way to make it work, most people couldn't possibly do what we'd done.

Also, we'd learned more over time about the whole mini pig/baby pig switcheroo. It seems that I'm hardly the only one to fall for that. Turns out people get screwed the way we did *all the time.* It would be funny if it didn't turn out so horribly in practice, because almost every other time it happens, it turns out very badly for the pigs. They get sent to shelters. Some end up being euthanized. We felt an obligation to warn people so they didn't make the same mistake we did.

Our story ended up on the second page of the *Star*. And it wasn't just the stamp-sized picture and a couple of sentences as we'd feared—it was a gorgeous, prominent, amazing story. You can't *buy* that kind of publicity. It's like having a massive audience on prime-time television while simultaneously being the top trend on Twitter. And the response was just as epic. The next thing we knew, two Canadian television networks—City and Global—wanted to cover Esther's story. By this point, we pretty much just said yes to everything. Hell, at that point the cat was out of the bag—or the pig was out of the poke, as it were.

After a while, it became old hat. We'd get the house clean and field the usual questions about how Esther had come into our lives and the effect she'd had on us and her huge (and quickly growing) base of followers. And every time when we thought life was starting to settle down into a new normal, something else would happen. It seemed like our story was everywhere. Our friends and family were freaked out that we were becoming quasi-celebrities based on the fact that we'd fallen in love with a pig. Regardless, it was clear the other shoe was about to drop: We'd just gone public in the most obvious ways, so we knew we'd have to move soon.

It was game over in Georgetown. It was just a matter of when.

Derek and I had talked about getting a farm. The more our lives changed, the more it started to make sense to us. It was still a dream, and a lofty one at that, but in the back of our minds we wondered if we could really make it work. What if we did buy a farm? What if we built a sanctuary so we could rescue lots of animals like Esther?

We decided to put up a post on our page to see what everybody thought. Esther's fans had been so involved in the entire story that we cared about their opinions. Also, in some subconscious way, I'm sure we wanted to give a large number of people the opportunity to provide us that "snap out of it" smack like Cher delivered to Nicolas Cage in the film *Moonstruck*. We needed that. Left to our own devices, you can see where we ended up: two men, two dogs, two cats, and a pig in a 1,000-square-foot house.

So we put up a post saying we were considering moving to the country, purchasing a farm, and turning it into a sanctuary. The response from Esther's fans was overwhelmingly positive. Also, a local real estate agent wrote to us, saying that her parents owned a pig farm, and she wanted to take us to see it.

Everything seemed to be falling into place. Maybe a bit too easily.

The agent took us to see the farm. I kind of liked it,

but Derek was underwhelmed. It was a long single-story barn. Honestly, it looked like a long, ugly house with a bungalow attached where *we* would live. It really wasn't very special, to put it very nicely. And I did need Derek to be the levelheaded one so I could see it more clearly. I think I was just excited by the idea of having some land. There was no urgency yet, so we left it alone for about a month.

We'd only seen that one underwhelming farm at that point, but even given that anticlimactic visit, we'd been bitten by the farm bug. So we decided to look at a few more.

When we found *the* farm, it was a total fluke. I was looking for listings to show a client and happened to be showing them a property two doors up. But when I was doing my searches, I came across a listing for Cedar Brook Farm. My clients were looking in a price range Derek and I hadn't considered before, almost $300,000 over our budget. The farm certainly wasn't something I would show my clients. But I found myself reading the description anyway, telling myself, "I'll just take a peek at these photos," knowing in the back of my mind I was on a mission. What I didn't expect was for the photos to reveal everything I could ever have wanted for Derek and me, and from the photos alone, price be damned: I knew I had to show it to Derek.

Prior to that point, even when we talked about it on Facebook, the idea of owning or operating a sanctuary was nothing more than a dream. It was a wonderful dream, but at best, it was something we thought we might try to tackle someday far in the future. Not at this point in our lives.

Those photos, though.

I couldn't get it out of my head. (And a farm is a very large thing to have stuck in your head.)

I printed out the listing itself and made a special trip to the office to print the farm's photos in color. Then I came home and handed the printouts to Derek.

"We need to see this," I said.

I watched Derek look over the listing and carefully examine the photographs, his eyes widening. Was that a twinkle in his eye?

Then I heard him scoff.

Yeah, there's the other shoe dropping. He's looking at the price.

He looked up at me the way a parent looks at a child whose face is covered with chocolate and crumbs and who swears he did not eat that piece of cake. I knew that look. But I also knew that twinkle. And for whatever reason, he relented and agreed to take a drive with me that morning to "just check it out."

"This is not going to be another Georgetown," he said.

And I knew exactly what he meant. Before we bought the Georgetown house, I had been showing the property to another client, but I called Derek and told him I'd found our house and that he needed to come over right away. He did, and we bought it that night.

"The location is amazing," I said, and he agreed that it was.

The price? Less amazing.

To be fair, I probably didn't expect it to be as perfect in real life, because nothing ever is. I knew the farm could be like a date with someone you met on the Internet. The object of your affections seems so clever in online communications and the photos look amazing. When you meet in person, it turns out the photo was ten years old and taken from that one good angle that hides the lazy eye and hideous hairline. Oh, and the person is three inches shorter and forty pounds heavier than advertised—and has the personality of a rice cake.

Only this Internet date was like if George Clooney and Megan Fox had a baby. Indescribably perfect. And now I had the agony of knowing how much we loved it and how there was no way in hell we could afford it.

And I needed it.

I was in love.

(I know. I do that a lot. Just work with me here.)

The minute we pulled up the driveway, the property seemed magical. From the winding driveway that crossed a stream to the thick forest that blocked the buildings from the road, plus the centuries-old stone walls that divided the fifty-acre property from end to end, it was breathtaking.

We hadn't even gotten out of the car when we turned to each other and said, "This is it." Sometimes you just know in life. Like when I first laid eyes on Derek or when that Facebook "friend" said, *Do you know anyone who might want a mini pig?* We knew this was our farm.

The barn was a filthy mess—cobwebs hanging up to three feet from the ceiling—and it had apparently become a storage/junk collection space. There were no fences other than the collapsing stone walls, but it had so much potential. The house was solid and clean, but it couldn't have been further from our style. Nor did it have things we thought all houses had, like a furnace for heat. As you recall, we're not huge fans of freezing our asses off. But it wasn't about the house or the barn or the fences (or lack thereof). There was just something about the property itself we both immediately fell in love with. And even though, cosmetically, it needed a ton of work, we both knew it was perfect.

Surprisingly, Derek was ready to jump immediately. I, however, was terrified about the cost. *What happened to "This is not going to be another Georgetown?"* Now I was the one starting to think more responsibly. (Who would have thought?) It was definitely more than we needed, by a lot. But as we were making these big life changes to accommodate our new life with Esther, it just started making sense. Whatever its flaws, this would be a great place to create an animal sanctuary. If you looked at Derek and me and what our lives at the time were all about, this made no sense at all. But with one pig's smile and the encouragement of thousands of strangers, somehow this made perfect sense.

We felt like this was our opportunity to—as cheesy as it sounds—do our part to change the world. (Like I said, work with me.) We really thought we could make a difference, and it felt like anything was possible.

We would have been happy to move into a little house on a few acres and just keep doing what we were doing with Esther, but we had been presented with this opportunity to maybe do something so much bigger. So how could we pass it up, no matter how scary it was?

Then again, maybe we were delusional, because everybody in our life and their brother thought we were nuts. I can imagine what they were thinking: *You're two guys and a pig. How do you think you're going to raise the half a million dollars you'd need to actually buy this place?* (And that's presuming we could get the owners to even consider such a low offer.)

But then we posted the idea on Esther's Facebook page as a hypothetical. (We liked treating the page sort of like a Magic 8 Ball.) We told them we'd found something we loved, but we explained the situation about the cost. We floated the idea of turning it into a sanctuary, and the Comment feed lit up like we had never seen before. Private message after private message came flying in telling us to go for it: *We've got your back. Follow your hearts. You know you can do this. You got this, yes!* (And every other possible iteration of *affirmative*.) It was a seemingly never-ending series of the most uplifting and reassuring comments you can imagine. We essentially had a hundred thousand cheerleaders making us think this was possible. People were coming from every direction, offering to contribute and help us do it, and that's how the idea of a crowdfunding campaign came to be.

We figured we had no choice but to throw an offer out there and see what happened. If they accepted it, we would figure out the next steps. If not, at least we tried. It was the reaction from the Facebook page that made us think we might actually be able to do something bigger than what we had initially thought.

So yeah, we drank the Kool-Aid.

Things moved fast, which I'm sure is no surprise. When I decide to do something, I can't stand any grass growing under my feet. Call it a strength; call it a weakness—sometimes it's both wrapped up in an enchilada—but I'm all about immediate action. So the time between Derek and my visiting the farm, discussing the idea, asking the fans, and actually making the offer was negligible. It all went down in just three days. The support from the page was enough for us to feel like we could do this, and that gave us the courage to put in an offer at their asking price but with a sixty-day conditional hold to close on the property.

I knew damn well that the offer was totally unacceptable when I put it in. Remember, I work in real estate, and I know asking for sixty days is ridiculous, especially in the best real estate market possible. We'd be asking them to take the farm off the market for two months when they'd told us there was already a competing offer in place. Yeah, there was also that to worry about. We might as well ask Bradley Cooper's agent whether he'd work for scale (the lowest possible rate) to star in a film of Esther's life story. In the role of Esther.

I explained all that to Derek as I prepared the paperwork. I guess I was trying to soften the blow for him (and for myself) if they rejected it. But that was the only offer we could make. We didn't have four hundred grand in our back pocket, and that was the number we'd decided we would need for a down payment to make paying off the rest of the farm possible. It's funny how things like "reality" set in when you're in the quiet of your mind and not delusional from the eternal optimism of a hundred thousand strangers (all of whom we love, but none of whom had accepted the responsibility, at least at that time, of paying for this farm).

I just wanted us to brace ourselves, because we had really fallen hard for the farm. Once Derek and I sat down and had a heart-to-heart, we agreed that we truly didn't think the owners would accept the offer, but we had to give it a shot. If we didn't, we'd always think in the back of our minds, *Remember that perfect farm? What if we'd made an offer and they'd said yes?*

When the offer was ready to be presented, I knew because it was a competition—and because Derek and I were so emotional—that I wouldn't be able to present it the way I wanted to. I asked the listing agent if I could fax a cover letter with the offer so the farm owners could know a little about us.

In the cover letter, we told our story. We explained why we had come to look at Cedar Brook, how much we'd fallen in love with it, and what we planned to do with it. We just laid all our cards on the table in the hopes that they'd like the idea and would want to be supportive. I wanted to tug at the heartstrings a little so they'd see this wasn't just a piece of property to us—this was our game-changer. This was how we were going to make a difference.

We needed them to know this wasn't going to be a situation where we wanted to tear the farm down and build a McMansion. Cedar Brook was in a big development area. We figured the other people looking at it would probably tear it down and turn it into a subdivision.

They'd sell it off for big estate houses—that's what people were doing in the area.

But we wanted to keep the farm a farm. We wanted to keep all the character it had, and we hoped that would matter to the owners—especially since we would only be the third unrelated owners of the farm since it was settled in 1860. If they went with someone else, all the history more than likely would be gone.

Then came the matter of the deposit. We had only $5,000 to put down. Again, that was absurd, and we knew it. That's the kind of deposit offer you'd make on a $200,000 house. So we were coming in with this ridiculous pittance of cash *and* asking them to hold it for sixty days while we tried to determine whether we could come up with the money for the actual down payment. If you're a gambler, you do not bet on those odds. You pack up what's left of your chips, tip the dealer, and go home. (Always tip your dealer and servers, folks. That's just good karma.)

Picture it: You walk up to someone trying to sell their house and say, *Hey, I really like your house and I want to buy it, but I've got no money and I'd need to raise a half a million dollars to be able to do this. So...could you please wait sixty days while I try to do this impossible thing?* Nobody in their right mind says yes to that. (Especially when they had that other offer from people who might have had all cash—we didn't know.)

It wasn't just our lowball $5,000 deposit that made it such a joke of an offer. It was the combination of that with the extended conditional hold so nobody else could have it. That last part was the killer. The five grand was just insult to injury. (And yes, I realize that we were the ones doing the insulting and injuring in this case, but remember: It's only a metaphor.)

I've been selling houses for eleven years and never in my life have I seen someone accept an offer like the one we proposed. We offered supplemental deposits, but those were conditional upon our raising the money and doing what we were hoping and were telling them we could do. And then they had to take the leap of faith that we could get our shit together in a matter of days. Good luck.

And then... believe it or not...

They accepted our offer!

(Sure, of course you believe it, because there's no way this story was ending with *They told us to fuck off, so now we live in a double-wide trailer behind a Walmart.* But put yourself in our shoes for the moment.)

We were in complete shock when they said yes. They called to tell us they had changed *next to nothing* in our offer. They made a couple of small revisions, such as adjusting our closing date, and basically left everything else alone. Their changes were nothing that would make a difference in whether we forged ahead, so now the ball was in our court.

Well.

Shit.

Now we actually have to deal with this situation.

You know that saying, *Be careful what you wish for?* Well, there we were.

It's sort of like walking right up to the prettiest guy in school, or girl in school (or whatever gender you're into—you get it), and asking that person out. There's no way on earth you're expecting a yes, so there's nothing to lose! Well, except your pride, but you knew you'd get rejected anyway, so it's no biggie. It's not like you're devastated when you buy a single lottery ticket and don't win a million dollars.

That's how we felt. We'd asked out the dreamboat, and now we actually had to take out the dreamboat. And this wasn't just a date: This was a marriage proposal.

We literally only had a couple of hours to decide whether we were going to sign the deal and be bound to the offer...or let our dream farm go. Plus, Esther had a cold.

Derek and I were both a bit freaked out. Suddenly everything became *real*. How were we going to get this money? The minute the owners said yes, the money clock started ticking: We had to figure out how we were going to do it.

We'd thought all along about the crowdfunding

campaign. We'd seen everybody else do one—hell, one guy on the Internet built a crowdfunding campaign to make macaroni and cheese (and did very well)! We had a *way* better angle than that.

The only issue, of course, was that we had exactly *zero* knowledge of how to build a crowdfunding campaign.

We didn't know where to begin or what site to use. There were so many to choose from: Kickstarter, Indiegogo, GoFundMe, HelpMeBuyaSandwich.com—you name it. (Okay, we ruled out the last one pretty early on.) We didn't know which one to use, how to set one up, what the expenses were.

The other big question: How much do we ask for? Two hundred thousand? Four hundred thousand? Six hundred thousand? And holy crap, we'd better get going.

Shit got really fucking real right about then. We'd just started the process of purchasing something we couldn't afford. We were putting ourselves in a position to lose everything if we didn't do this properly. Our mortgage was about to triple. Animals need to eat. How many could we rescue? The questions were endless and it seemed like we had minutes to make every decision because it was happening so fast.

We decided to set the goal at $400,000 and to launch the campaign with Indiegogo because it had the most flexibility. Kickstarter wouldn't let us fund something that involved purchasing real estate, and if we launched the campaign there and didn't meet the goal, all the money would be returned to the donors. Indiegogo had next to no restrictions. They charged 3 percent if we hit our target and 9 percent if we didn't. But Indiegogo also had something called "flexible funding": If we didn't hit the target, we'd still get the money we'd raised—we'd just have to pay out that higher percentage fee.

We figured if we set a goal for $400,000 and the campaign ended with us at $375,000, we could still find a way to make it work. Having to start from scratch if we didn't hit the target seemed like too much to ask of people, and that was the bottom line when choosing which site to use: the one that would piss off people the least.

Esther's fans rallied like crazy from the moment we launched the campaign. By the end of day one we hit $30,000. For the first couple of weeks, the donations climbed steadily. Three weeks in, we were at $160,000, which was amazing. At that point, donations stalled a bit, which was concerning. But we knew there were ways to reinvigorate the campaign, such as refreshing perks and adding new ones, so we started to do that to keep it interesting. If someone had given twenty dollars for a twenty-dollar perk, we'd change the perk so maybe it would entice them to give another twenty dollars. We tried to keep the campaign evolving and to respond to what people were buying.

At the same time, we were pursuing the real-life things we had to do to fulfill our end of the offer's conditions. We had the sixty-day contingency to get the finances, but we only had a week to do inspections and nail down insurance. There were a whole bunch of other steps we needed to complete to get the offer moving forward. At no time was there just one thing on the table. We were still trying to balance the rest of our life as well, and Esther's cold— if that's what it actually was—was getting worse.

She was lying on the couch, trembling like a leaf, which was every bit as upsetting as you can imagine a trembling Esther would be. We think of her as our big, strong, happy girl. To see her so vulnerable, weak and shaking like that threw us into a tailspin entirely separate from the campaign. She'd even stopped eating and drinking. (*Very* unlike our girl.)

We'd heard that pigs sometimes eat ice in winter conditions and that if they eat too much of it, the ice can throw their internal temperature out of whack, causing fevers or shock to set in. You freak out when you seek out answers on WebMD about any of your own health concerns, but when it's your kid (or your pig), you freak out that much more and imagine the worst. (And you know me by now. If anyone's going to freak out, it's me.)

Esther could have eaten the equivalent of a twelve-foot ice sculpture for all I knew, and after a couple days of her quivering on the couch, one thing was certain:

We had to take her temperature. Her ears and belly were super hot and really pink—pinker than normal—and her snout was beaded with sweat, so she really looked like she was suffering from a fever. Never having had to take a commercial pig's temperature before, we didn't happen to own a commercial pig thermometer. (In retrospect, that was an oversight.)

So Derek and I took one for the team, as it were. We sacrificed our personal thermometer.

You can see where this is going. We lubed it up, and while the queen was sleeping...we slid it right up in there. The first time we did this, it went off without a hitch. The thermometer confirmed that she *did* have a fever, so we started giving her juice to keep her hydrated. (This wound up helping her get better, but it also kind of screwed us, because this is when she stopped drinking plain water and she never drank it again.) We realized that Esther's condition was the flu.

The second time we attempted to take her temperature was less easy breezy. Esther was definitely on the mend by then, and she did not take kindly to having anything inserted in her caboose! She shot off like an out-of-control Mack truck—down the hall and into the office. She might as well have slammed the shutters and flipped up a CLOSED FOR BUSINESS sign.

Meanwhile, back on the campaign front, an anonymous

donor offered to match all donations up to $50,000 over a two-day period. Can you imagine? Talk about an incredible offer! So we made that announcement and the donations came in like crazy.

As wonderful as that seemed at first, the plan ran into a big hiccup: Several weeks went by without our receiving the matching donor's money. People were watching the numbers on the campaign and when they didn't see that extra $50,000 from the donor, it made us look like liars. Nobody actually came out and made that accusation, but we knew what it looked like, and I think people started to question what was going on. (That's totally understandable in retrospect, but it was a huge kick to the gut at the time.) So once again the donations started to stall.

It was a dark time. The idea of Esther's fans' losing faith in us made us start to lose hope and feel like failures. All those people who'd said we were crazy...were they going to be right? We started to question ourselves. Maybe we *were* nuts. Maybe we *couldn't* do this.

It was scary for a while. Derek and I relied on each other and our faith that if we kept believing, if we kept at it, things would work out. It wasn't easy, but we did our best to be vigilant. We knew we were doing the right thing. We knew we had a lot of people counting on us. We knew we had to find a way to make this happen.

Or we could just say screw it and run off to the Bahamas.

Okay, I'm just kidding. We weren't going to do that. But it sure seemed tempting!

At least Esther was on the mend. Now we just needed our little campaign to follow suit.

And just as Esther's flu cleared up to the point that she was again getting into mischief, the matching donor money *finally* arrived for real. It bumped the donation total over $240,000 and *completely* reignited the campaign. Still, we only had a few weeks left, and a huge gap remained.

On June 28, two days before the campaign was going to close, Derek woke me up, holding his phone in my face.

We were at $404,000. *We'd done it.* And like every other completely insane thing that had happened to us over the past year, once again we were like, *Holy shit— this is happening.*

Right up to that morning, we still had an out. We could say we weren't actually going to purchase the farm for any number of reasons, either real or contrived: the farm didn't accept the offer, the campaign failed and we couldn't get the money, whatever. But we'd done it.

Of course, this was scary in its own way—scarier than anything we'd dealt with before. We had just committed ourselves to millions of people who were watching online. In that moment it became official, literally and figuratively. There was no shutting this down anymore. We'd done it.

We'd *literally* bought the farm.

We'd have to sell our house and move. Up until that point it had still been a far-off dream, something neat to watch unfold, but it wasn't real. Now, even if we wanted to go back, we couldn't. We'd told people we were doing this; we'd taken money for it, so now we had to do it.

Almost everybody had thought it was impossible. Even people who supported us had had their doubts. If you tasked some of the biggest organizations in the world with raising half a million dollars in two months, they'd struggle. And we certainly were no big organization. We were just Derek and Steve and our dream for Happily Ever Esther. And we did it.

I'd never felt anything like it in my life. I went within three seconds from tears of happiness to tears of terror. And occasionally back again. We'd felt so inconsequential before any of this. Esther's existence had gotten the attention of people from all over the world, and now here we were setting off to make our mark. But more important, we had a purpose. A real purpose. We were going to save countless animals and give them a home and a life that would not otherwise have been possible. That was everything.

It was crazy to think how much our lives had changed since Esther had entered them. As hokey as it sounds, even when you think you have the most unsurpassable challenge in front of you, you can do it. Three years ago, we'd never have thought this possible. And yet...

CHAPTER EIGHT

O ne of the most popular T-shirts we offer in the Esther Store on our website reads: EAT. SLEEP. ROOT. REPEAT. Because those are Esther's favorite things to do, most often in that order. (But you'd really have to ask her if you want to know for sure.) The *root* in *eat, sleep, root, repeat* is non-negotiable when it comes to Esther's lifestyle. A girl's gotta root. For the uninitiated, rooting essentially involves Esther's digging her snout as deep as she can into the grass and sod, flipping it over, and then moving an inch to the left or right (depending on her mood) and digging another hole. She roots. This is what she does. She's going to root at any given time during any given day. Multiple times.

Dogs bury things. Cats sharpen their claws (on *everything*). Chickens cluck, snakes slither, meerkats . . . okay, I have no idea what meerkats do, but it's probably something adorable. You get the point. Animals do what's in their nature, and rooting is what pigs do. Hence the slogan.

Over the course of the previous two years, Esther absolutely destroyed our grass. Because we wanted to make everything look nice for Esther's birthday party, we'd put new sod in the backyard in July. That way the lawn would look nice for our guests. Makes sense, right? We didn't consider that there would be at least two months between the party and selling the house. You'd think as we were getting the house together, it might have occurred to us that we probably should *not* have put new sod in the backyard until the *very* last few days we were going to be there.

Well, it didn't.

Which brings us back to the slogan, and whereas the *eat* and *sleep* didn't create issues, the *root* and *repeat* sure did. Just two months after we'd replaced all the sod in the backyard, it looked like we'd done virtually nothing to fix it. Esther just rooted the shit out of it. Such is the power of Esther. We weren't upset at her, of course. She was just doing her job, following the instincts directly wired into her genetic coding. Instincts that demanded she completely fuck up the backyard. But what was done was done, and we needed to do our best to mitigate the damage as we readied to sell the house.

For the two weeks before we had our first showings, I was constantly out back, rolling the sod Esther had flipped over, trying to get it to take. I would spend forty-five minutes fixing everything up until the yard looked pristine. I'd go back in the house, tired but content in a job well done. The next time I'd look out the window, there would be ten pieces of sod flipped upside down. And the same would happen to Derek after he'd spent some time out there making things look nice. Esther would go outside and play Whack-a-Mole in reverse.

Getting sod to take is a process; you have to water it so the roots will grow, but all the watering makes it soft, so having a 600-pound ballerina dancing around the yard when you're trying to establish healthy roots definitely complicates the process. There were holes everywhere. We might as well have dug foxholes and put in bunkers, because the yard looked like a war zone. All the topsoil we'd put down ended up just making a mushy mess. (I must say, it *was* gorgeous as of the actual night of the party. Just not, you know, before or after that night.)

On the day we were finally hosting our agent open house, we also had seven showings scheduled. They were scattered throughout the day, so there was really no good time to bring Esther back into the house or the backyard. That meant she and Derek were stuck in the storage container, which we'd haphazardly jammed full of all of our boxes and belongings.

We'd had so many wonderful times in our home. Just like people who raise children in a home have fond memories, we felt that way about having raised our pets there. This was where our animals had grown up, had all their adventures, and brought so much joy into our lives. This was the house Esther had come home to when she was only as big as a sneaker. We wanted the buyer to love the house.

As the day trudged on and buyer after buyer seemed less than enthused, we started to worry. But then visitor number seven showed up and she loved the house, the yard—she said she loved everything about it and thought it was a perfect fit for her. It made us so happy to know the house was going to someone who seemed so kind and who would appreciate it. All this woman needed to do was her home inspection and her financing—all standard stuff. She wanted a November closing, but she said she was flexible on that. Our closing date on the house was set for November 10, and our closing day on the farm was November 6. That was perfect: It gave us a few days' bridge to make the move before closing on the sale. All we had left to do was the inspection, and what could go wrong? (Besides everything.) We'd been so charmed all along the way it just felt like the other shoe had to drop, and in the pit of my stomach, I was sure that would happen during the inspection.

But it didn't.

Of course, we had to hide Esther for the inspection. I mean, there's no real way to "hide" Esther, but we had to bounce her around a bit and keep her outside so she'd be out of the way. Which would be an excellent strategy, but like a kid whose idea of recreation is playing Xbox all day, Esther doesn't like to be outside for extended periods of time. (What is she, an animal?) Esther thinks of herself as a person, and a person doesn't want to be outside all the time. She lives in a house and enjoys her outside time, but when she wants in, she wants in. And when she doesn't get her way . . . she's vocal.

So here we were having the home inspected, and Esther started roaring like a jetliner, demanding to be let in. But we were finally at a place where it didn't matter—we were moving. We could breathe a sigh of relief and just let her scream. Which is not to say we were neglecting her; we just didn't have that panicked feeling we'd always had in the past that we'd be discovered and get in trouble, forcing us to do anything we could to keep her quiet. This time, we just let her scream. Which some might say is healthy. Who *doesn't* want to just scream for about twenty minutes every now and then?

As we got into the move full-force, really boxing things up and emptying the house out, Esther started to get unsettled. If you own pets, you know how it is. Animals pick up on change. She knew something was up. It all started to happen really quickly once the house was sold. There was a clear change in her behavior. She'd look out the window and watch our every move. If we set down a new box, she'd knock it over to see what was in it. She'd scrutinize every time we were coming or going. She'd watch for people pulling up and things leaving the house. Suddenly she'd become a guard pig better than any guard dog you could ever ask for (and much, *much* bigger).

This was something she'd never experienced before. Sure, she'd never had any use for that lamp in the corner, but now she'd look at us like, *Where the hell are you taking that lamp?* Or we'd leave for extended periods of time because we had lawyer appointments and other business taking place outside of the house, and when we returned, Esther's typical easygoing attitude had been replaced by a curious, anxious one. She might as well have had her arms crossed, toes tapping out an angry little beat to the tune of *And where were you, Mister?* In the past, if she ever seemed unsettled, we'd give her a couple of mints and she'd do her thing where she sucks the floor. After a bit, she'd chill out and go to bed. But the mints weren't cutting it that week.

She started pacing a lot more than usual and wanted to come into our room more than ever. She would be aggressive about trying to get into our bedroom when the door was locked. She definitely paid more attention to us and what we did. And because we weren't doing anything that seemed normal (like hanging out in the living room watching TV), she was really nervous. But we were busy! We were packing and organizing in the basement, and we still had to move a ton of stuff out of there. She quickly took note of that too.

The house had split stairs, so Esther would walk down the first set of stairs, turn herself around on the landing, and stand there, peering down the next set of stairs at us, tossing out the occasional honk. We had to keep an eye on her because the minute she'd take one step down, one of us would have to rush over and usher her back up. That was because we didn't know whether we'd ever be able to get her back upstairs again if she got herself down into the basement. She'd grown a lot since her last time down there, and we sure weren't going to risk it. The staircase had open risers, so I was always terrified one of Esther's legs would slip through the opening and she'd fall and break her legs. So one of us would escort her back up and then go into the kitchen and shake her jar of mints. That's the Esther bell. When she hears us shake the jar, she knows to come for a mint. It has a 100 percent success rate. Just like you can immediately find all of your cats by running the electric can opener (*Tuna alert!*), shaking the mint jar immediately produces one very excited Esther. But it was a repetitive process. We'd get back down into the basement and start to get a groove on, thinking Esther was calm and going to lie down, but then we'd hear her footsteps. First came the steps down the hallway, then the steps on the stairs, and Derek and I would look at each other like, *Okay, whose turn is it?*

There was never a dull moment. But that's how it

always was with Esther. She wasn't always this nervous, of course, because we weren't always packing up all of our belongings. But it wasn't like things were exactly tranquil before. Even if I was just sitting at the computer doing something, I'd often have to type with one hand because Esther wanted to nuzzle my other hand. (Anyone who owns a computer and at least one cat knows how this process works.) We always had one ear on Esther, kind of like you would with a toddler. A very, very, large toddler who could potentially flip the stove over to get at something left up there.

This was also the first time that we took Esther out front intentionally. We wanted to get a photo of her with the SOLD sign. Nothing terribly exciting happened in that moment, but it was exciting for us. Before then, we'd always felt the need to hide her. But that day we marched her out front, posed her by the sign, and took a happy photo to post on the page for all of her fans. It was a great feeling. The house had always been Esther's home too (sometimes even more than it was ours), and now she was able to stand proudly out front. Sure, that's only because we were selling the house, but so what? It was the close of a massive chapter in our life with Esther—and of course, the beginning of an exciting new one.

I was so distracted by everything that had been going on, I didn't even realize the date and actually wasn't

even expecting the lawyer's call. When I saw our lawyer's name on caller ID, I wondered why she was calling.
I don't know why, but it took me by surprise that it was a
done deal and she was calling me to come get the keys.
There had just been so much going on, and we had been
that little engine going *I think I can* for so long that it
was uncanny to have finally made it over the mountain.
Was someone going to wake me up now? Was this all a
dream?

I felt so many different emotions in that moment. I
didn't know if I was going to burst into tears or laughter...or some kind of victorious battle cry. And since I
didn't quite know how to process the depth and breadth
of my feelings, I just sneaked out of the house to pick
up the keys. If closing day had caught *me*, a real estate
professional, by surprise, maybe the same was true of
Derek. And now I could give him the gift of something
wonderful and unexpected by surprising him when I
came home.

In a perfect world—or even a pretty average world,
frankly, but dammit, I was busy—I'd have come up with
some clever way to announce that it was official, that
the farm was ours. Perhaps I could have annoyed Derek
with a scavenger hunt that eventually led to the keys. Or
I could have pretended I'd left something in the other
room and asked Derek to get it for me, and when he
walked in: *Boom!* Farm keys! Were I the magician in

the family, I could have pulled a quarter from behind Derek's ear—only it's not a quarter, it's the farm keys!

But I did none of those things. I just ran into the house like an excited idiot shouting, "I've got the keys, I've got the keys!" I waved the keys in the air, just in case I hadn't been clear enough with my words.

This is what a set of keys looks like!

Also, jazz hands!

We went straight to the farm. (We did not pass Go; we did not collect two hundred dollars.) It was me and Derek and Shelby and Reuben. It was the first time we'd ever stepped onto the property with nobody else there. Every other time, we'd been with family or friends or real estate agents or photographers, but this time it was just us. At our farm.

I cried like a baby. (Like you were expecting anything else, right?)

We walked the dogs through the house and explored everything. The dogs hadn't been there before, so this was a completely new experience for them, and you know how dogs are when they're exploring someplace new—they're completely fascinated. It hadn't really occurred to me before what an amazing gift this was for them too: a whole new adventure, with so many new sights to see and smells to investigate and rooms to do their thing—it made me so happy to see the excitement in their eyes.

We ran around as they ran around, from this room

to that one, then outside and through the trailer. All we wanted to do was look at everything and explore every nook and cranny, but at the same time, the new home-owner thing was kicking in. We knew we also needed to check everything to make sure things were working properly, that nothing had been taken that shouldn't have been, that the previous owners had left everything they said they'd leave. It turned out we had no reason to worry. Not only did they do everything they said they would, they even left us some little extras and sweet notes for us. For instance, they left us a metal cart, a replica of a machine the husband used when he worked at the railroad. When he retired, the company made him a metal replica of his machine and filled it with little replica farm animals. They were apparently giving him a little joshing about the fact that he was retiring to become a farmer—but it so happened that they put a *pig* in the driver's seat. How perfect could this be? Story of our life, right? The pig was at the wheel in total control of everything. It was a perfect little metaphor for what our lives had become.

We couldn't believe the farm was ours. We didn't care that the house needed work or that this thing or that thing would need to be fixed or built or painted; we didn't care about anything except the fact that it was *ours*. This was so much more than we had ever thought we'd have at our age and at this point in our lives. It was what everybody wants to have someday: their little piece of the countryside, or their loft in the city, or their beach house—their little place of paradise, whatever it may be. This was our version of paradise. And we had it.

And of course, the most important consideration: We were going to *do good with it*. We were going to rescue countless animals in need. This wouldn't just be *our* home; it would be a home to all sorts of animals, a place where basic needs like food and shelter would be met, of course, but a place that offered so much more: care, love, appreciation, affection, *hope*.

It's one thing to set foot on your new property, in your new home, and think of all the wonders it has in store for you and your family. And of course we were feeling all of that. But it's a whole other level to think of welcoming all these animals in need to your new home. We would be their sanctuary. We would be the light at the end of the tunnel. Animals who had been abused, neglected, mistreated—and God knows it's excruciating to even think of all the terrible ways some so-called human beings can treat these lovely, innocent creatures—we would offer them salvation. And it was all because Esther's story had touched so many wonderful people, people who had come together to help make this dream a reality.

Derek and I told each other all the standard mushy things you'd think we'd say. We hugged and jumped up and down and took turns crying and sometimes cried at the same time. We were starting over, together. And it was an unbelievable feeling. As we walked the property, we kept happening across little things. We'd say, "I never noticed that," or "I've never seen this part of the property before," and we knew it would be forever before we saw it all and really got to know the entire property. That was part of the thrill. We knew the adventure and the possibilities it represented. There was so much to discover: The sky truly was the limit with this farm.

The following day, we got the truck. Esther was completely out of sorts, partly because four of us—my mom, my stepdad, Derek, and I—spent most of that day building a fence to keep Esther in her pasture. We had to have that done before we brought Esther to the farm, and we had to bring Esther the next day because we'd planned Set Me Free for November 8.

Set Me Free was the name we came up with for when everyone would get to see Esther walk into the field at her new home. That was also one of the perks we'd added to the Indiegogo campaign, so a lot of Esther's fans were making the trip to welcome her to the sanctuary. And we were also having a little thank-you party for everyone who had helped us along the way and everyone who made the trip. Because that date was locked in—we couldn't very well tell people coming here from all over that we needed a few extra days—we only had one day to build the fence. We got it done thanks to our determination and a lot of sweat, but that didn't mean Esther was happy about being left alone all day.

When we got back, Esther had moved her bed to the middle of the living room, the carpet was completely screwed up—folded up like an accordion—and she was lying down completely out of place (like everything else), resting her head on the newly bundled carpet like it was a pillow. I can imagine her thought process: *Everything else is out of sorts, fuck it, I'm moving shit too.*

I expected to be an emotional mess leading up to (and during) the whole move, but a weird numb feeling had set in. I almost felt like what was happening wasn't real. I kept thinking back about everything and how quickly this had all transpired, and I couldn't wrap my head around it. Of course, even while mostly numb, I still had a few little moments of panic-induced emotion over the house itself and the whole scenario in general. One moment I remember in particular occurred a few days before the move. I was pulling onto our street, and got ready to make that right turn into our driveway, and I randomly thought: *This is one of the last times I'll pull in this way to go home.* It left me feeling overwhelmed with sadness. The big move was exciting, of course, but before any of this had happened, we'd had no intention of *ever* moving!

Before this all came about, I'd had grand plans for an addition and all kinds of renovations. The house was our first, and we'd thought we would be in it for years before we even considered moving to our dream house in the country. Wow, were we wrong. So as I pulled up and looked at the grass out front and our front steps, it just washed over me. I suddenly realized I was sobbing like a baby.

Things were moving at such a rapid pace that neither Derek nor I really had time to sit down and discuss our feelings. That's the downside of always just going right at it when we want to do something, I guess. It's worked out well for us, but it doesn't leave much opportunity for reflection. It was always *What's next? Where do we need to be? Is the lawyer sorted? Is the bank sorted?* It was nothing but business all the time. And because I still had a lot of financial concerns about what we were getting into, I was trying not to let my productivity at work wane in any way. I needed to know we had a healthy cushion and weren't running into this adventure broke.

To be clear, things were moving *so* fast. As in crazy fast. The party would be happening at the farm just two days after we took possession and before we actually moved out of our house. And yes, this goes back to that issue of planning that always turns out to be a sticking point for me. We got the keys to the farm four days before we had to leave the Georgetown house, which seemed like plenty of time originally, but it turned out to be madness every single day.

The day before the official move was the busiest. We had friends over throughout the day, some helping pack, others running errands for us, darting in and out to pick up party supplies, and helping finish up the thank-you party plans. By the time everyone went home and we had a chance to sit down, the house looked pretty barren. The rugs were rolled up, the stereo was boxed up with pictures, and many previously packed boxes were scattered on the counters and dining room table. We used a lot of newspaper to wrap breakables, so that was also littered in little piles around the house.

Derek and I ate our dinner and watched *King of the Hill* on my laptop, neither of us really even talking, but both of us deep in thought. Occasionally one of us would say something, but it was just the odd question about timing: who was driving what, stuff like that, just going over details. I think we both knew that if we actually said, *This is it. This chapter of our life is over*, we'd both start crying. The day I cried in the car hadn't been the only time, and I'm certain Derek cried a few times when I wasn't around. It's funny how we sometimes hide our vulnerabilities even though they bring us closer when we reveal them. After a full day of packing, neither of us had the energy for all that emotion.

We never got a chance to have a goodbye toast of champagne or a candlelight dinner. It was heated soup over cardboard boxes and wadded-up pieces of newspaper—super classy and romantic. We went to bed fairly early that night, partly because we were physically exhausted, partly because the next few days would be chaos as we tried to get somewhat settled before Esther arrived a few days later.

As soon as we got the keys, we moved as much as we could to the farm, started building the fence for Esther, and began to set up for the party. Why we thought it was a good idea to throw a party mere hours after the move is anyone's guess. (Fine. You don't even need to guess. You've surely noticed that I don't completely think things through from time to time. Or ever.) Most of our stuff was packed, but we were going to have one more night in the house. Esther was to move the next day, and once that happened we wouldn't be spending the night there again. It felt bizarre. The couch was gone, as were most of the other large pieces of furniture, which meant we didn't have anything to sit on. But that was okay. Sitting on the floor with Esther and the dogs felt like we were camping inside our house. The cats were there too, but you know how cats are: They can't be bothered with stressful things like moving or packing. (Although the boxes themselves? They love a brand-new box like you just bought them a new car. *Mmmm, there's nothing like that new box smell.* It's the damnedest thing.) Cats live life on their own terms: They just want to be fed and petted, to have a clean litter box, and to occasionally make you look right at their butthole. (Which isn't to say there aren't people like this too, but when all is said and done, cats are the only ones who get away with this behavior over the long term.)

To be fair, Finnegan is more like a dog. He likes to be cuddled and doesn't have half of Delores's attitude. Delores has always been the bitchier cat. But both of them have a knack for going out at night and not coming home right away. (We have a "Don't ask, don't tell" policy about where they go and what they do.)

But on this night, we obviously couldn't risk that, so we locked them in the office, ensuring we could more easily crate them for the trip in the morning. You can just imagine how pleased Delores was about this. You might as well invite Charlie Sheen to a dry wedding reception.

We barely slept that night, for a couple of reasons: There was the obvious excitement about the next day— our first one really living at the farm—but we also were stressed out from all the horror stories we'd heard about moving livestock. Esther, as I might have mentioned once or twice or a hundred times, was a very big girl by this point, a full one-third of a ton. And this was going to be her first road trip. We'd been told it could be very stressful for her and a real challenge in so many ways. Our vet was coming along for the trip and would be on hand to tranquilize her if need be, but we didn't want to do that if at all possible. She was about to make her big debut! We didn't want her to be all doped up. We didn't want her to be like Farrah Fawcett the first time she was interviewed by David Letterman, all incoherent and out of it (though still glamorous). Everyone would be there. We wanted Esther to be Esther. So yes, we stayed up all night worrying about it.

CHAPTER NINE

I woke up on moving day with crazy anxiety—it might even have been my loud, exaggerated heartbeat that woke me up. By the time I opened my eyes, Derek was already awake, scurrying around since who knows when. It was probably somewhere between 7:30 and 8 a.m. before I rolled out of bed. I walked to the living room to survey what was left to do and heard Derek bustling around downstairs. Esther was still sleeping on her bed as usual. No panic for her. Just snoozing and snoring. As it turns out, ignorance really is bliss—even for pigs. Maybe especially for pigs.

I made my tea, checked email, all the typical morning things, but I couldn't settle down at all. I was hoping to relax a little for the moment, because I knew things would get crazy as soon as the movers showed up. But I had zero chill at that time. It turned out that Derek was similarly anxious: That was why he was in the basement, randomly shuffling boxes to pass the time. When I gave up on relaxing, I joined him in the basement, but shortly thereafter we heard the telltale clicking of hooves on the floor, alerting us that the queen was up and ready for breakfast. Picture her in a robe, yawning and stretching, pointing a hoof toward the kitchen as if to say, *Chop chop, gentlemen. Breakfast is the most important meal of the day.* (For the record: All meals are equally important to this not-so-little piggy.)

By the time I got back upstairs, she was already in the kitchen, waiting for me to feed her. And by the time I got to the kitchen, she was positioned in front of the fridge, honking away. She knows the morning routine, and it's my job to make sure there are only a few short moments between when I hear that pitter-patter of hooves and when I have delivered *madame's* breakfast. Any deviation results in some "hurry it up" honking.

Once she'd devoured her meal, Esther and I went outside. I leaned against our back door with my tea, watching Esther do her thing. I knew it was her last morning in our yard. It was my last morning in our yard. I stood there with tears in my eyes, tears that came from two very different sources: sad tears, because we were leaving our house, and happy tears, because I knew we could do so much better for Esther at the new farm. It was nice to have a few minutes to myself and I took advantage of them, remembering special moments, all of the firsts, reminiscing before I'd even gone. Regardless of how magical our destination was, I was going to miss this place. I didn't talk to anyone. I didn't check my messages. I just stood there, took a few deep breaths, and after about ten minutes, wandered back inside to get myself ready.

By now it was shortly after nine o'clock, and Derek had moved from relatively calm basement shuffling to near-panicked darting around the main floor. He was prepping our bags for the day, checking his notes, and calling the vet to make sure everyone was on schedule. People started trickling in as we were running around, doing whatever we could as we waited for the trailer to arrive. The semi-calm (although anxious) feeling of the morning was quickly fading and becoming more chaotic and loud as people gathered and chatted. Everyone was excited and (of course) incredibly happy for us, but I think all Derek and I really wanted was to enjoy the moment. Unfortunately, with so many people around, that part was kind of lost. We spent the majority of our remaining time in the house answering people's questions. They all just wanted to help, but it was lot of *Do you want me to bring this?* or *What time are we leaving?* or *Do you want me to lead?* I appreciated how caring they were, but at the same time, those were questions that really didn't matter to me at the time. All we wanted to do was ensure that Esther was safely moved, along with the rest of our "furkids." Everything else was irrelevant at that time.

Amid the chatter and excitement inside, I noticed the trailer arrive. I didn't say anything to anyone; I just quietly slipped out the back door. Esther was still outside at this point, so I went to the backyard with her and took her over to the fence.

"Hey, Esther," I said, as I pointed to the trailer. I knelt beside her and stroked her back. "We're going to go out front in a few minutes and get into that trailer."

She looked toward the trailer and blinked her eyes, then turned her gaze back to me.

"I'm going to be with you the whole time," I said, and as I began my next sentence, my voice cracked. "We're going to a farm. A big, beautiful, magical farm."

I don't know if she understood me, but her expressive eyes showed me *something*.

"I love you so much, sweet girl."

I was full-on crying as I finished my speech to a pig—something that probably makes me seem crazy. But I was trying to explain what was happening and what was going to happen. In case she *did* understand.

A number of times that day, I felt like I was an observer in the entire process rather than a participant. And even as an observer, it was like I was detached from everything that was going on, almost as if I were watching it in a movie. I'm not going to say I had an out-of-body experience or anything outrageous like that, but it was a very surreal, almost hazy feeling. I know I was there, but I also feel like I watched it all from above. People would be talking, but I would fade in and out of hearing what they said. I was too distracted by my own thoughts, which were going about a mile a minute and gaining speed the closer we got to loading Esther onto the trailer.

We had a four-car escort for our trip. There was our vet, my mom and stepdad, my sister, and the brilliant photographer Jo-Anne McArthur—she was there to take photos and document our move. The cats were in crates and in the car by 9:30. We got the dogs in the car, and then it was time to move our big girl.

We had no idea how this was going to go. We spent some time with her outside in the garden to calm her nerves before the attempt. I just tried to occupy her because there were so many doors opening and closing and people arriving. I wanted to let her root and do a little bit of her natural routine at least one last time.

Much to our surprise, it took less than five minutes to get Esther into the trailer. Derek and I hopped in there, shook some kibble, and gave her an apple...and she climbed right up! We were shocked, considering all the warnings we'd been given, but relieved that it happened so easily.

We'd warned the transport company that we would have to be in the trailer with Esther when we made the trip. Apparently it's technically illegal for a person to be in the trailer when traveling with livestock, but we told the driver ahead of time that if we weren't allowed in the back we'd find another driver, so the company built us a four-foot-tall wall in the trailer as a safe zone in case Esther freaked. (Of course Esther would never hurt us intentionally, but you never know what might happen if she panicked.)

As they started to close the doors to the trailer, one of our friends asked, "Well, how do you feel?"

"I don't even know what to say," Derek began, and then he started to cry. I reached over and hugged him, and we laughed together. (I might have made fun of him for blubbering because that's my typical coping mechanism, but then they closed the doors.) And off to the farm we went...

The only other contents of the trailer were hay and Esther's mattress and blanket. We wanted her to be comfortable, of course. And she spent the entire trip on that mattress. Standing. She stood on her bed the whole way, honking occasionally, turning around and pacing a little bit...but always on her bed. I stood the whole time too. A bit of solidarity there. This was the first time Derek and I had had a minute alone again, and we had a solid forty minutes with just the three of us. That's a fairly long trip for just two men in a trailer, much less two men and a pig who weighs a third of a ton and who has never been on a ride at her current size and age.

Derek was really stressed. I handle pressure better than he does. (Yes, really. Stop looking at me like that.)

"Are you okay?" I asked.

He nodded.

"Babe, we can do this," I said. "I know it's overwhelming, but we're on our way to an amazing new chapter. We're going to make a difference. We are going to help so many animals."

"How crazy is this?" he asked. "Did we really do this?"

"I think we did!"

We sure did—and if we'd forgotten, the bumpy ride in the back of the trailer reminded us. There was a tiny hole in the front of the trailer that I could peek out of to see outside, but I couldn't see where we were going except for that little slot. So I spent the whole trip looking out trying to figure out how close we were to our destination, usually guessing wrong.

For the rest of the ride, Esther was *such* a good girl. And then just as we were arriving, she turned and squatted and had a pee in the trailer. So she was 99 percent perfect and waited until literally thirty seconds before our arrival to let it go. I couldn't be mad about that. If someone suddenly took me on an entirely unexpected trip that ran forty minutes, depending on my condition at the time, I'm not so sure I could hold it either.

Despite the limited visibility, I actually *could* tell when we finally got onto our road because it's tar and gravel, not smooth pavement. Maybe Esther could tell too, given her decision to whiz away. We slowed down and made the turn into our driveway, and I could see the cedar trees going by and feel us going over the bridge. And I swear I'm not imagining this: Everything got brighter as we passed the trees and entered the clearing where the house and barn are. As we turned the corner onto the actual property, I could see all the people lined up outside the barn. It was an indescribable feeling to know that that was it: We were finally there.

I could see all kinds of people gathered there. I could hear people chatting and others telling them to keep it down so as not to startle Esther. We had told everybody in advance to be quiet when we arrived, because we didn't want Esther to get frightened. We pulled past the barn and straight into the pasture we had just fenced. It was time to introduce her to a real pasture, a real place for her to root and play and enjoy the great outdoors. My heart swelled.

When the trailer door opened, Esther just stood there, not knowing what to do with herself. But then Shelby came running around the back of the trailer to greet us, excited that we'd arrived, her tail wagging back and forth. As soon as Esther saw Shelby, she trotted right out of the trailer, much to the delight of everybody watching. We couldn't have scripted it better.

We let her explore for a minute or two before telling her to come along for a full-perimeter tour of the pasture. We did our stroll around the pasture adjacent to the barn. Esther just took it all in. Our guests stayed back and watched us walking Esther—just as we were letting Esther be and watching her take in this new place. It was invigorating to witness her exploring this field and following the dogs on this extensive walk. It was just like the vision we'd always had of taking Esther and the dogs for a real walk across a vast stretch of open pasture. And there she was, cruising around, happy as could be. It was so cool. The field was unkempt, so it was waist-high grass that was wet from rain that morning, and we all got soaked, but nobody seemed to care. We walked around for a solid hour, even running at times, as Esther explored this massive new space.

Then we finally headed back toward the barn. That's where we got to say hello to all our guests, many of whom were contributors to the Indiegogo campaign. We'd already cried plenty when we were loading Esther into the trailer, so you'd think we'd have been all cried out by this point. (Actually, forget that: You know better by now.) Derek turned to everyone who had come to the house to help us that morning. He started to say thank you, but he couldn't even get through it before he burst into tears.

Still, all things considered, we were relatively calm once we got to the farm—not overly emotional in front of our guests. Plus we were a bit shell-shocked and in a bit of a haze. But we were so excited and relieved to finally have Esther there and know she was safe.

Of course she'd always been safe with us in our house in Georgetown, but now she was *really* safe. She was no longer living somewhere she wasn't allowed to be. We didn't have to hide her. We didn't have to worry about what would happen if she were discovered, that we might lose her. This was her home, and she could roam it freely and happily and *proudly*. It was such a feeling of relief. A gigantic weight had been lifted off our shoulders, and even though you'd think Esther wouldn't feel it—she didn't know she was essentially a refugee from the industrial food complex, as good as a fugitive on the lam, hiding away for years—it seemed like she knew she was truly free for the first time. Like I said, pigs are smart. And Esther's as smart as any pig you'll find.

Once everyone had left, Derek went back to Georgetown and returned to packing the few remaining things while I stayed at the farm with Esther and the critter contingent, slowly starting to get us all settled at the new house. When Derek finally got back late that night, we had a glass of wine and went for a short walk outside, just us and the dogs. Esther was already asleep in the living room on our mattress, so we took the opportunity to just breathe and look around in awe at our new surroundings.

Of course, if I said all our worries were gone from that point forward, you wouldn't believe me anyway. That's not my nature. We'd accomplished a lot, but soon what

ESTHER THE WONDER PIG

we had done really sank in, and the worries resurfaced. This was the end of one chapter but the beginning of such a new and entirely different one. It was the beginning of the sanctuary itself. Who knew what this would bring? This was something we'd never done before. How were we going to actually make it work?

We were realizing that getting here had actually been the easy part. Now the real work was going to start. But this was our new life. Every amazing and wonderful thing that happened to us was because of an animal that most people don't think of as more than a barcode in a grocery store. I never could have dreamed that one decision to take in a tiny pig—who would eventually be an anything-but-tiny pig—would change our lives so completely. And more to the point, that Esther would change so many other lives in the process.

Now we had our Happily Ever Esther. We might have adopted Esther, but the "kindness is contagious" attitude that we adopted *from* Esther had changed our entire life.

All because we'd fallen in love with a pig and her smile.

EPILOGUE

For most people, completing a move like this would be the end game; for us, it was just the beginning. Getting the farm was only the start of Esther's mission. She had changed our lives—that's obvious. She taught us how to be the people we are today. She showed us how to love unconditionally, and she showed us how powerful a smile could be.

Dr. Paul Farmer said it best: "The idea that some lives matter less is the root of all that's wrong with the world." Esther helped us see the truth in that statement.

So now it's our turn to try to change the world for the rest of the Esthers out there.

Once we completed the move, Derek and I finally had a few days more or less to ourselves. I really wish I could say we had that quiet and romantic "We made it!" moment, but quiet isn't something we do, and our version of romance is the comfort of sitting beside each other, watching mindless TV with our faces buried in our phones.

With that said, we definitely (and repeatedly) had some magical moments of *Look babe, this is our farm!* These occurred while we walked around the property with Esther, reminding each other of all the amazing things that had happened over the previous ten months, all while daydreaming about what the future was going to look like.

And that future was now. Our conversations upon moving went almost immediately to *What's next? We're here. Now what do we do?* And we couldn't wait to get started.

We look at each other every day in disbelief at the kindness of strangers and with a newfound belief in miracles. We hadn't found Esther. She'd found us, and that led to us finding our calling.

We all like to think that we're doing the best we can, but what does that even mean? And who are we "doing the best we can" for? At some point, we need to take a step back and realize there might be a whole lot more to this world than we realize. Esther is a prime example of that. Just because we (like pretty much everyone else) spent our entire lives thinking something was okay, that doesn't mean it actually *was.* Since our relationship with Esther opened our eyes, it's become our mission to show the world what Esther has taught us, and to teach everyone that all of us can become kinder and more open-minded. Maybe our story will show people the amazing things you can accomplish when you believe in yourself and really go for it, even when—hell, *especially* when— others tell you something is impossible.

We definitely doubted ourselves every step of the way, and we took turns freaking out and pulling each other back from the edge, but we did it. Derek and I did so many things we never, not in a million years, thought we would do. We didn't think we could live an "Esther Approved" lifestyle, but we did it. We didn't think we could raise a 650-pound pig in our house, but we did it. And we surely didn't think we could rally thousands of people from around the world to help us buy and build a farm sanctuary, but we did it. Kindness is magic, and Esther is proof that a smile can change the world.

Life today is definitely different. For starters, it's really dark on the farm at night, and I am apparently terrified of the dark. So even nine months into our new life, I still sprint like Usain Bolt running the 100-meter dash when I need to go from my car to the house. I had no idea I could run so fast.

I also never expected to have piglet afterbirth on my hands on April Fools' Day, of all times. No, Esther didn't get knocked up. She's a proper lady. We rescued a pregnant pig who gave birth to a quintet of adorable little squeakers, and it was no prank—but at least her timing suggested she had a sense of humor about the whole thing. So now we have five beautiful piglets who will live out their lives with their mother (whom we named April) by their side.

It's hard to believe that a little over a year earlier this had all been nothing more than a far-fetched dream. I look around in awe and still pinch myself every day to make sure it actually came true.

As of this writing, we have provided a safe home to thirty-three animals: six rabbits, six goats, two sheep, ten pigs (not including Esther), one horse, one donkey, three cows, three chickens, and a peacock. That's in addition to our original five beloved pets. And we have requests to take in new residents almost every day. By the time you're reading this, the number will have grown. And we look forward to welcoming even more residents to our farm, where they can all live "Happily Ever Esther."

RECIPES

Black Bean Tacos with Homemade Cashew Sour Cream

Taco Ingredients:

1 13-ounce can black beans, drained and rinsed

2 cups salsa*

8 soft tortillas (corn or wheat)

2 avocados, diced

2 tomatoes, chopped

1 lime, cut into 8 slices

1 handful of cilantro, chopped

* Use your favorite store-bought variety, or a homemade recipe you are already familiar with.

Taco Directions:

- Place the beans and ½ cup of the salsa in a saucepan and heat over medium-low heat until they are warm. Set aside.
- Warm tortillas according to package directions.
- In each warm tortilla place a heaping spoonful of each of the warm bean and salsa mixture, avocado, salsa, and tomato. Squirt some fresh lime juice on top, and then bring it home with a healthy dollop of Cashew Sour Cream (see below) and garnish with cilantro.

Cashew Sour Cream Ingredients:

1 cup cashews
½ cup water (not the cashew-soaking water)
Juice of ½ lemon
½ teaspoon apple cider vinegar

Cashew Sour Cream Directions:

- Place the cashews in a bowl of water, making sure they are covered by the water, and let them soak for 4 hours. Drain and rinse cashews and place in a blender with the remaining ingredients. Blend until smooth.

Makes 8 tacos

CASHEW DILL CHEESE

Ingredients:

1 cup raw cashews

¼ cup nutritional yeast

1 teaspoon sea salt

1 teaspoon onion powder

1 cup water

1 teaspoon agar powder

¼ cup chopped fresh dill

Directions:

- Lightly grease 6 spaces in your muffin tin using vegetable oil like sunflower or safflower.
- Place the cashews, nutritional yeast, salt, and onion powder in a blender or food processor and process until you have a fine cashew texture (not a cashew butter).
- Heat water in a small saucepan to a boil and add the agar. Stir with a whisk and reduce the heat to a simmer, continually stirring for 5 minutes.
- Add the cashew mixture into the agar and water mixture and stir with whisk to fully combine. Then add the dill and stir a few times.
- Spoon the mixture into the 6 muffin tin spaces and place in the fridge. Let the cheese set for about an

hour uncovered in the fridge and then turn out the cheese onto a plate and enjoy!

- **Tips and Tricks:** Sub out the dill and onion powder and try adding your own flavors and spices. For instance, use a store-bought taco mix and instead of allowing the cheese to set in the fridge, serve warm as a nacho dip. (My personal favorite.)

SAVORY HOLIDAY STUFFING

Ingredients:

3 tablespoons vegan butter or vegetable oil

1 onion, chopped

1 green pepper, chopped

10 mushrooms, sliced

4 stalks celery, finely chopped

2 cloves garlic, finely chopped

½ loaf rye or gluten-free bread, toasted and cut into small cubes

1 cup vegetable stock

3 tablespoons tamari

1½ teaspoons poultry seasoning

Pepper to taste

Directions:

- Heat up a large frying pan over medium heat, and add the vegan butter or vegetable oil and the onion. Sauté until onion is clear. Stir in the green pepper, mushrooms, celery, and garlic. Cook for a few minutes and then add the cubed bread, vegetable stock, tamari, poultry seasoning, and pepper. Continue to sauté until the bread absorbs all of the liquid. Remove from heat and cover with foil to keep moist until serving.

Serves 4–5

TOMATO LENTIL CURRY SOUP

Ingredients:

4 cups vegetable broth

2 cups water

1 onion, chopped

2 cloves garlic, chopped

1 winter squash,* peeled, seeded, and cubed

1 5.5-ounce can tomato paste

1 sweet potato, cubed

3 carrots, chopped

(continued)

* Types of winter squash include buttercup, butternut, acorn, and so on. Use your favorite!

½ cup red lentils

1 tablespoon curry powder, or more if you like it spicy

Directions:

— Pour ¼ cup of the vegetable broth or of the water into a soup pot over medium heat and add onion and garlic. Simmer for about 5 minutes. Add the remaining ingredients, including the rest of the broth and water, cover, and bring to a boil. Reduce to a simmer and cook for 30 minutes more.

Serves 4

SMOKED TLT WRAP

Ingredients:

½ tablespoon Bragg Liquid Aminos or any soy sauce

¼ package of smoked tofu,* thinly sliced

1 tablespoon eggless mayonnaise (such as Vegenaise or Just Mayo)

Pepper to taste

1 tortilla (flour or gluten-free)

1 handful of lettuce

½ tomato, sliced

* Smoked tofu can be found in most health food stores and in a lot of grocery stores. Regular firm tofu can be used as an alternative.

Directions:

- In a pan over medium heat, add the Liquid Aminos or soy sauce and the smoked tofu and fry for just a couple of minutes. This will make your smoked tofu taste amazing.
- Spread the eggless mayo (with pepper added to taste) over half the tortilla, add lettuce, tomato, and fried tofu slices, and roll the tortilla up like a burrito.

Makes 1 wrap

VANILLA CASHEW MILK

Ingredients:

1 cup raw cashews
5 cups water (not the cashew-soaking water)
3 dates, pitted
1 teaspoon vanilla extract

Directions:

— Place the cashews in a bowl of water, making sure they are covered by the water, and let them soak overnight or for a minimum of 4 hours. Drain and rinse. Place all ingredients in a blender and blend for 1 minute or until smooth. Use the milky goodness within a week.

Makes 4½ cups

NUTTY CHOCOLATE ICE CREAM BARS

Ice Cream Ingredients:

1 13-ounce can full-fat coconut milk

4 tablespoons maple syrup

1 teaspoon vanilla extract

Chocolate Coating Ingredients:

2½ tablespoons maple syrup

2½ tablespoons coconut oil

2½ tablespoons cocoa or raw cacao

¼ cup almonds or pecans, finely chopped

1 pinch of sea salt

Directions:

- Refrigerate the unopened can of coconut milk for at least 3 hours or overnight, so the cream rises to the top inside the can. Once chilled, open the can and remove the firm cream, which will be at the top of the can, leaving the coconut water behind. (You can save the coconut water for another purpose, such as using it in your next smoothie.)
- Place the coconut cream, maple syrup, and vanilla extract in a blender or food processor and blend until smooth. Pour into 4 small Popsicle molds, insert the Popsicle stick, and freeze for at least 2 hours, until frozen solid.
- When the bars are frozen, combine maple syrup, coconut oil, cocoa, nuts, and sea salt in a small pot over medium heat. Stir until coconut oil is melted and everything is well mixed. Set pot aside to cool for about 20 minutes.
- Remove frozen ice cream bars from their molds and cover with chocolate coating using a knife the way you would ice a cake. Place the bars on a plate or tray lined with parchment paper and return to the freezer for 20 minutes or until chocolate coating has hardened.
- I dare you to eat just one.

Makes 4 small ice cream bars

HOMEMADE CHOCOLATE TURTLES

Ingredients:

   12 soft, fresh dates (such as medjool), pitted

   1 tablespoon vanilla extract

   1 cup pecans halves

   ¾ cup dairy-free chocolate (semi-sweet chocolate chips
      or a couple of dark chocolate bars)

Directions:

   — Place the dates and vanilla extract in a bowl and mix
     together with your hands. You want to soften the
     dates and mix in the vanilla flavor. Form 30 small
     balls about the size of a large marble and then slightly
     flatten them. These will be your "caramel" centers.

   — Cut two pecan halves lengthwise to form the four
     legs and stick one end of each piece into the cara-
     mel center. Use the rounded end of one half of a
     pecan for the turtle head.

   — Melt the chocolate in a double boiler or very care-
     fully in a small pot over low heat, stirring continu-
     ously so it does not burn. Once melted, remove
     from heat.

   — Place a dab of melted chocolate on the bottom of
     the turtle. This will help hold the legs and head
     in place. Set the turtle bottom side down on tray
     covered with a sheet of parchment paper. Dab with

melted chocolate to cover the top of the turtle. Repeat the process of adding pecans and melted chocolate to the rest of the caramel centers. Once all the turtles are formed, place in the fridge to set.

Makes 30 turtles

CHOCOLATE PEANUT BUTTER PIE

Ingredients:

½ cup natural peanut butter
1 prepared graham cracker pie crust (such as Keebler Ready Crust Graham Pie Crust)
1 cup dairy-free chocolate chips
15–20 ounces soft or silken, non-GMO tofu, drained
½ cup sugar
¼ teaspoon sea salt
1 teaspoon vanilla extract

Directions:

- Preheat oven to 350 degrees Fahrenheit.
- Spoon peanut butter into graham cracker pie crust and spread gently to cover the base of the crust.
- Melt chocolate chips in a saucepan over low heat. Transfer melted chocolate to a blender and add tofu, sugar, sea salt, and vanilla extract. Blend

until smooth. Pour over peanut butter in prepared pie crust and bake 40 minutes. Allow to cool and then place in fridge for approximately 1 hour to chill before serving. Can also be served frozen, if desired.

Serves 6

ESTHER-APPROVED CHERRY CHEESECAKE

Ingredients:

- ½ pound soft or silken tofu
- 1 approximately 8-ounce tub of Tofutti Better Than Cream Cheese
- ¾ cup sugar
- Juice of ½ lemon
- 1 teaspoon vanilla extract
- 1 prepared graham cracker pie crust (such as Keebler Ready Crust Graham Pie Crust)
- 1 10-ounce can cherry pie filling

Directions:

- Preheat oven to 350 degrees Fahrenheit.
- Place the tofu, Tofutti cream cheese, sugar, lemon juice, and vanilla extract in a blender and blend until smooth. Pour into graham cracker crust. Bake

40–45 minutes. The filling will look firm and the crust will begin to brown. Allow to cool slightly and then refrigerate until completely cool. Top with cherry pie filling and serve.

Serves 6

TOASTED COCONUT TAHINI CHOCOLATE CHIP COOKIES

Ingredients:

1 tablespoon ground chia or ground flaxseeds for making chia or flax egg*

3 tablespoons water for the chia egg, plus 1–2 tablespoons more for the final mixing of the dough

1⅓ cups oat flour (You can simply grind rolled oats in a blender, food processor, or coffee grinder to make the flour.)

½ teaspoon baking soda

½ teaspoon sea salt

½ cup tahini

½ teaspoon vanilla extract

(continued)

* To make 1 chia or flax egg, combine 1 tablespoon of the seeds with 3 tablespoons of water in a small bowl. Let the mixture sit for 10 minutes until it becomes gelatinous.

½ cup sugar (best with less-processed and unbleached sugar such as unrefined brown sugar or Sucanat)

½ cup dairy-free chocolate chips

½ cup toasted coconut (toasted in dry frying pan or toaster oven)

1–2 tablespoons water, as needed when doing the final mixing

Directions:

- Preheat the oven to 350 degrees Fahrenheit.
- Make 1 chia or flax egg.
- In a large bowl add the flour, baking soda, and salt and stir until combined.
- In a smaller bowl combine the tahini, vanilla extract, and sugar and stir until combined.
- Add the wet ingredients from the small bowl and the chia or flax egg into the dry ingredients of the large bowl and stir until well mixed. (You may want to consider using your hands to combine these ingredients as it really speeds things up). Add the chocolate chips and toasted coconut and mix until well combined. If the mixture seems too dry, feel free to add 1–2 tablespoons of extra water here to help the cookie dough come together.
- Form each cookie by creating a ball with about 2 tablespoons of the cookie dough and then pressing it into a cookie shape on a baking sheet lined

with parchment paper. The cookies will not spread much, so create them in the shape you would like to see them when they come out of the oven.

— Bake for 12–14 minutes or until they begin to brown.

Makes 12 cookies

ACKNOWLEDGMENTS

Thanks to:

Our parents and siblings. Your unwavering love and support of our dreams, no matter how crazy they may have seemed, are the reason we are the men we are today.

Our amazing circle of friends. For always being there for us and for understanding and supporting us no matter what we do. Our adventures wouldn't be the same without you.

Dr. David Kirkham and the staff at Cheltenham Veterinary Centre. For never being too busy to take our calls and answer our countless crazy questions, no matter the time of day.

Caprice Crane. For turning our thoughts and stories into something we will treasure for the rest of our lives. There isn't enough room on this page to express how much we appreciate your help, your patience, your sense of humor, and your friendship.

Erica Silverman, our agent. We can't imagine having anyone else help us navigate this strange and sometimes overwhelming world of writing a book. Thank you for helping us make sense of it all, and for being our guide on this amazing adventure.

Lauren Plude and Libby Burton, our editors. For believing we had a story worth telling, and for helping us make sure it was told our way.

And the countless people we have met on this incredible journey. You shared your stories and gave us the motivation we needed to keep going, even when we doubted ourselves.

This book would not have been possible if it were not for each and every one of you.

ABOUT THE AUTHORS

STEVE JENKINS was working as a Realtor and living with his partner, DEREK WALTER, a professional magician, when their life was flipped upside down thanks to a beloved pet pig named Esther. Never ones to back down from a challenge, Steve and Derek buckled up for the ride of a lifetime, turning "Esther the Wonder Pig" into a social media powerhouse. In just two short years, Steve and Derek have cemented a place for themselves among the world's most well-known and successful animal activists, accumulating hundreds of thousands of followers all over the world. In 2014, Steve and Derek founded the Happily Ever Esther Farm Sanctuary in Campbellville, Ontario, where they continue to rescue and rehabilitate abandoned and abused farmed animals.

CAPRICE CRANE is an award-winning, internationally bestselling, five-time novelist, screenwriter, and television writer with her finger on the pulse of pop culture. With a voice noted for being as witty as it is relatable,

Caprice's humor and satirical observations have earned her a wildly loyal social media following and the distinction as one of the Huffington Post's "50 Funny People You Should Be Following on Twitter."

Her debut novel *Stupid and Contagious* was published in fourteen countries and Caprice was awarded the 2006 RT Reviewers' Choice Award. She followed that success in 2007 by winning the same award with her equally clever and comedic second novel, *Forget about It*, another international bestseller. She's since published three more novels to critical acclaim including her debut YA novel, *Confessions of a Hater*, which received a love letter in the *New York Times* Book Review in fall of 2013.

A veteran of TV writing, Caprice had her first feature film released by IFC Films in 2011, and she sold a television pilot to NBC that same year. She's since sold pilots to CBS and 20th Century Fox and a feature film to the Hallmark channel, and she continues to write books and screenplays and to develop programs for TV.

Her first love is her sixteen-year-old Shih Tzu, Max, who is both blind and deaf, which she says could be why their relationship has lasted so long. All she's ever wanted to do is make people laugh, because life can be painful but also hilarious. She tries to find the humor in the pain and firmly believes that the best offense is a good sense of humor.